Contents

I0800993

Dedication

For Bentley

And his friends on the other side
Buster, BJ, and Rufus

Acknowledgments

I am so blessed that all of my friends love animals as much as I do, and many of them take that love a step farther, and work with animals on the metaphysical plain as well. I want to thank Dinah Roseberry, Victoria Gross, Rev. Tim Shaw, Kenny Kingston and Willie Windwalker Gibson for sharing their wisdom.

Introduction

According to historians, there is no record as to when we began keeping animals as pets, although DOGS were most likely the first pets because they have been domesticated for about 10,000 years.

The ancient Romans are known to have kept pets, particularly DOGS and BIRDS. CATS and HORSES were also popular with Romans and may have been considered pets, but they were also working animals. The origins of ornamental GOLDFISH date back to the seventh century in China, where Buddhist monks first raised them in ponds. By the fourteenth century the Chinese were keeping GOLDFISH indoors in bowls as pets.

In ancient Egypt, CATS were considered demigods and the property of the divine Pharaoh. That ranked them above humans, making them the first to be saved if a house caught fire. The penalty for taking the life of a greyhound was the same as that of killing a man.

Early on, some DOGS, CATS, and BIRDS were referred to as pets, but also performed useful tasks such as guarding the house and killing RATS. In that vein, tropical BIRDS, such as PARROTS, were highly valued in American society before recorded music became available.

The modern age of pet keeping began in the mid-1800s, when a thriving middle class emerged. This was the first time that many people had the time and money to keep animals solely for companionship and pleasure.

Way back when, in the Pagan world, witches adopted certain animals as their own link to nature spirits and deities. Wizards, magicians, and village healers used them to diagnose illnesses, sources of bewitchment, divination, and to find lost property or treasure.

It was not until the Middle Ages and the rise of Christianity that the witches' pets and animals became thought of as agents of evil. As the persecution of witches began, the church started teaching the concept that the Witches' familiar was an associate of the Christian devil. They became demons and evil spirits in animal form, sent out by the witch to do their malevolent bidding. They also believed witches possessed the power to transform themselves into animals, in which guise they committed any number of diabolical deeds. Later, they were believed to use animal products in spells, making potions and concoctions to aid transformation, gain power over nature, or even to harm and kill. Many pet CATS were put to death with their owners on suspicion of witchcraft.

The most common animals associated with witchcraft were the: FROG, OWL, SERPENT, PIG, RAVEN, STAG, GOAT, WOLF, DOG, HORSE, BAT, MOUSE and of course the CAT, but any animal, REPTILE or INSECT could be suspect. Obsession with the witches' familiar was most prevalent in England and Scotland and was mentioned in numerous trial records of the period.

According to the ancient Witchcraft Act of 1604, it was a felony to "consult, covenant with, entertain, employ, feed or reward any evil or wicked spirit to or for any intent or purpose..."

"Matthew Hopkins," the infamous Witch Finder General used this act with zeal when extracting confessions. He also used the "Malleus Malificarum," the so-called Inquisitor's Handbook. Though it offers no instruction concerning familiars in the interrogation and trial of witches, it does acknowledge that an animal familiar "always works with the witch in everything..." As such, it advised the inquisitor never to leave a witch prisoner alone, "or the devil will cause him or her to kill themselves, accomplished through a familiar."

With this in mind, Hopkins would tie the witch up in a cell and leave them alone, while watching secretly for the animal's arrival. If so much as a FLY or BEETLE approached them, it was deemed proof enough that they were indeed witches.

In contemporary witchcraft, the thought of animals as demonic spirits of evil does not exist, but many still use animals when working with magick. Animals are welcomed into the magick circle when power is being raised or spells are being cast. They are also used to aid scrying, divination, and spirit contact. When working with magick, animals act as a guard in psychic defense because they visibly react to negative forces and harmful energy.

Now there is a big difference in using animals in spell work and doing spells for and about them, and that's what this book is about; spells for animals both domesticated and wild.

There are also a few chapters written by some very good friends of mine talking about Animal Communication, Divination and Animals, Animal Healing, and Pet Grief—and a whole lot more.

Most of us love our pets as our own children and want the best for them always. It is my hope that by writing this book, we will all be able to return that unconditional love that they give us every day in many wonderful ways.

Blessed Be to you and all the furry, winged or scaled critters in your lives.

Animal Superstitions

Almost all of us are superstitious in one way or another, and animals play a big role in feeding many of those fears. Some of the superstitions below are laughable, others are just common sense, and some are reasons to take heed.

Bats

To the Chinese and Poles, BATS are a good omen of long life and happiness.

If a BAT lands on your head, you should hope the CRICKET sees rain coming because the BAT won't get off until it hears thunder.

When you see a BAT, you might actually be seeing the Devil, a witch, a ghost, or Dracula.

BATS have always had a connection with witches, and can have good or bad connotations, depending on the tradition. According to one, if a BAT flies three times around a house, it is a death omen. Conversely, when BATS come out early and fly about playfully, it is a sign of good weather to come.

Bear

BEARS only mate once every seven years, and when they do, they cause such a disturbance in the atmosphere that any pregnant cattle in the district will give birth to still-born CALVES.

Naming a BEAR provokes attack.

Birds

A bird that flies into a house, foretells an important message.

The white bird foretells death.

A bird call from the north means tragedy; from the south is good for crops; from the west is good luck; from the east, good love.

If a bird poops on you or your car, it is a sign of good luck.

Crows

One's bad,
Two's luck,
Three's health,
Four's wealth,
Five's sickness,
Six is death.

Cats

If a cat sneezes, it is a sign of rain. If a cat sneezes three times, a cold will run through the family. If a cat sneezes near a bride, it means she will have good luck in her wedded life.

Cats can be harbingers of coming prosperity and good fortune. A cat of three colors is extremely lucky and will keep a house from harm, while a smutty-nosed cat will bring wealth to its companions. Stroking a cat's tail nine times grants good luck at cards. And just sharing your home with cats will bring you many blessings.

A Norse legend tells of the chariot of Freya, the witch, that was pulled by black cats that transformed into black horses. They were exceedingly swift and surely possessed by the Devil. After serving Freya for seven years, the cats were rewarded by being turned into witches, disguised as black cats. This seems to have led to the belief in the Middle Ages that black cats were familiars of witches.

The Norse believed if a black cat crossed your path, Satan was taking notice of you.

Butter your cat's feet when you move to keep it from running away from the new house.

If a cat crosses or jumps over the coffin, the dead person's spirit will return as a ghost.

In Ancient Egypt, it was bad luck to kill a cat. Anyone who did was put to death.

In Egypt, it was believed that a black cat crossing one's path brought good luck.

In East Anglia, England, they used to mummify cats and place them in the walls of their homes to ward off evil spirits.

If a black cat walks towards you, it brings good fortune, but if it walks away, it takes your good luck with it.

Keep cats away from babies because they "suck the breath" of the child.

A cat onboard a ship is considered to bring luck.

A kitten born in May is considered to be a witches cat, or "familiar."

A white cat crossing your path brings good luck.

Coming upon a stray tortoise shell cat is a bad omen.

Cats bought with money will never be good mousers.

A cat washing itself on the doorstep will bring a visit from the clergy.

Killing a cat is sacrificing your soul to the Devil.

Kicking a CAT brings on rheumatism.

A CAT sneezing is a good omen for everyone who hears it.

It is bad luck to see a white CAT at night, however, dreaming of white CAT means good luck.

When you see a one-eyed CAT, spit on your thumb, stamp it in the palm of your hand, and make a wish. The wish will come true.

If a CAT washes behind its ears, it will rain.

A CAT sleeping with all four paws tucked under means cold weather ahead.

Crossing a stream with a CAT will bring bad luck.

Sleeping with a CAT will bring bad luck.

Dogs

It's good luck to meet a DOG, particularly a DALMATIAN.

It's bad luck to be followed by a strange DOG, particularly if it's black.

If a DOG howls three times, it means a death has occurred.

If a DOG howls for no reason, it indicates unseen spirits are around.

When a DOG eats grass, it means it's going to rain.

If a DOG passes between a couple who are going to be married, much ill-luck will result to them.

The Ancient Greeks thought DOGS could foresee evil.

If you have your newborn baby licked by a DOG, your baby will be a quick healer.

Howling DOGS mean the wind god has summoned death, and the spirits of the dead will be taken.

A howling DOG at night means bad luck or somebody close to you who will become very sick…or worse.

When a DOG is staring intently, at nothing, for no apparent reason, look between the DOG's ears and you'll see a ghost.

A howling DOG outside the house of a sick person was once thought to be an omen that the person would die, especially if the DOG was driven away and then returned to howl again.

A DOG that gives a single howl, or three howls, and then falls silent is said to be marking a death that has just occurred nearby.

DOGS were once used to cure illnesses. One old charm which was often used for children's illnesses was to take some of the patient's hairs and feed them to a DOG in between slices of bread and butter; the ailment was believed to transfer to the animal, healing the patient.

In Scotland, a strange DOG coming to the house means a new friendship.

In England, to meet a spotted or black and white DOG on your way to a business appointment is lucky.

Three white DOGS seen together are considered lucky in some areas.

Fishermen traditionally regard DOGS as unlucky and will not take one out in a boat, or mention the word "DOG" whilst at sea.

South Dakota Lakota Sioux Indians claim that if a member of the tribe would get sick, they would lay with a DOG and the sickness would transfer from the tribal member into the DOG. On some of the reservations, among the elders, this practice is still being used.

Dolphin

Dolphins are believed to transport the souls of the dead to the afterlife.

Dolphins playing in fine weather or close to the shore means windy conditions.

Donkey

Christian tradition stated that donkeys originally had unmarked hides, and that it was only after Christ's entry into Jerusalem on the back of a donkey that they received the dark cross on their backs. The hairs from the cross were widely believed to cure a number of ailments, and were often worn in a charm around the neck to guard against whooping-cough, toothache, fits, and to ease teething pains in babies. Sometimes the hairs were eaten in a sandwich instead.

Riding a donkey was believed efficacious, especially if the rider faced the donkey's tail end, and was sometimes used as a preventative for toothache, measles and other children's complaints.

One cure for whooping-cough and ague stated that the patient should be passed under a donkey and over its back either three or nine times; the trick of feeding an animal some of the patient's hair to transfer the illness was also used with donkeys.

The donkey was also used to help cure the complaints of other animals; letting a black donkey run with mares in a field was thought to stop the mares miscarrying.

There is also a tradition that to see a dead donkey means great good fortune, and even as recently as this century it was considered a good-luck charm to leap over the carcass of a dead donkey three times.

When a donkey brays and twitches its ears, it is said to be an omen that there will be wet weather.

ELEPHANTS

In Siam, white ELEPHANTS were rare and not made to work for their upkeep, so a White ELEPHANT is an item that is a non-profit expense. That's why items kept as memorabilia could be considered White ELEPHANTS.

FISH

Throw back the first FISH you catch then you'll be lucky the whole day fishing.

It's bad luck to get married when the FISH aren't biting, according to some customs.

If you dream of FISH, someone you know is pregnant.

If you count the number of FISH you caught, you will catch no more that day.

It's bad luck to say the word "PIG" while fishing at sea.

FROGS

FROGS, like TOADS, were once thought to have peculiar properties, and were frequently used in healing charms.

A cure for thrush was to hold a live FROG with its head in the patient's mouth. As it breathed, so it drew the disease away and into itself.

Warts could also be cured by rubbing a FROG across them.

The dried body of a FROG worn in a silk bag around the neck averted epilepsy and other fits.

A FROG brings good luck to the house it enters.

Hens

A HEN which crows is considered to be unlucky, as is a HEN with tail-feathers like those of a ROOSTER. Those BIRDS would have been killed on most farms.

HENS which roost in the morning are said to be foretelling a death, usually that of the farmer or someone in his household.

A HEN that enters the house is an omen that a visitor will arrive, and this is also the case if a ROOSTER crows near the door or comes inside.

Horses

White HORSES are apparently an indication of bad luck. Upon meeting a white HORSE, one should spit and make a wish, or cross one's fingers until a DOG is seen.

It's considered bad luck to change a HORSE's name.

People who suffer from whooping cough will be cured by inhaling a HORSE's breath.

HORSE brasses were used to protect HORSES from witches.

A white HORSE could warn of danger, and lived longer than a dark HORSE, so was considered a living amulet against early death.

Spotted HORSES are magickal.

Grey HORSES and HORSES with four white socks are said to be unlucky.

HORSES were used as valuable sacrifices by many ancient peoples, including the Romans, and their bones were concealed in the walls of houses, or HORSE skulls placed on the gables of houses, as a protection.

In many places, it is lucky to lead a HORSE through the house; this belief may stem from the association of HORSES with fertility and crops, which has lasted in form of hobby-HORSES which were originally part of Beltane (May Day) revels.

HORSE-hairs, chopped very finely and fed to a child in bread and butter, were thought to be a certain cure for WORMS, and the HORSE-spurs (calluses which appear on the sides of a HORSE's leg) were believed in the eighteenth century to be a cure for cancer if dried, ground and drunk frequently with new milk.

Mouse

If somebody throws away a dead MOUSE, the wind will soon start to blow from that direction.

When MICE swarm into a house hitherto free from them, a member of the household will die.

To hear a MOUSE squeaking anywhere near someone who is ill is a sign that the person will die.

Much of the abhorrence towards MICE probably stems from the old superstition that they are the souls of people who have been murdered.

If a MOUSE nibbles anyone's clothing during the night, that person will suffer some misfortune.

No journey undertaken after seeing a MOUSE is likely to be successful.

MICE, minced, given to a sufferer, was said cure measles. Dried RAT's tails would cure a cold.

Pigs

To get rid of warts, rub a peeled apple on the wart than feed it to a PIG.

Rabbits

In the British Isles, before Christianity, the HARE, like the CAT, was thought to be a witch in disguise. This witch could only be killed with a silver bullet.

Since RABBITS and HARES were thought to be born with their eyes open, which is an erroneous notion, they supposedly had special powers over the evil eye.

It is believed to be unlucky to meet either a HARE or a RABBIT. A RABBIT which crosses one's path in front is a good omen and one which crosses behind is a bad one.

In some English counties it is considered unwise to shoot a black RABBIT, as it may be an ancestral spirit returning in RABBIT form.

In Suffolk, it was believed that white RABBITS were witches, therefore unlucky to shoot. RABBITS and HARES were never mentioned at sea, as they were considered ill-omened words, and to meet one on the way to sea was a very bad omen.

An old custom is to say "RABBITS" or "White RABBITS" either once or three times on the first day of the month as a good luck charm. It must be the first word said that morning, otherwise the charm is not effective.

Ravens

To kill a RAVEN is to harm the spirit of King Arthur who visits the world in the form of a raven.

It is said that the RAVEN, an ill-omened BIRD, is able to predict the future, particularly death.

If the RAVENS in the Tower of London should be lost or fly away, then the Royal Family will die and Britain will fall to an enemy.

Sheep

To meet a flock of SHEEP on a journey is an omen of good luck.

An old Manx belief states that SHEEP cannot be counted accurately unless the person counting them has washed his or her eyes under running water first.

Peaceful SHEEP, lying in the field, are said to herald fine weather, but rain is foretold if they are restless and baa for no apparent reason.

The knuckle-bone from a piece of mutton was once thought to be a preventative charm against rheumatism if carried in the pocket.

A certain T-shaped bone from a SHEEP's head was believed to protect its carrier from bad luck and evil.

A strip of sheepskin on a HORSE's collar was once used as a prevention against the evil eye.

A gruesome method of breaking a curse was to stick a SHEEP's heart full of pins and roast it at midnight in a room where all doors, windows, and openings had been firmly closed.

Parts of SHEEP were often used in folk cures. A SHEEP's lung was once applied to the feet of a pneumonia sufferer, and was thought to draw the disease downward into itself. People could be wrapped in the skin of a freshly-killed SHEEP in an attempt to cure an ADDER bite. Children with whooping-cough were thought to be cured by letting a SHEEP breathe on them. Sufferers from consumption were once advised to walk around a sheepfold many times a day, beginning early in the morning.

If SHEEP gnash their teeth during round-up in the autumn, the winter will be hard. If SHEEP gnash their teeth somewhere else, it presages very bad weather.

Weasels

It is impossible to catch a weasel asleep and it is bad luck if one crosses your path or appears near your home making its distinctive squeaking.

If a white weasel crosses your path, it presages death or misfortune; but if one runs in front of you, you will be able to beat all your enemies.

Wolf

During the middle ages, wolves were ascribed magical powers and wolf parts became an important part of many early pharmacies. Powdered wolf liver was used to ease birth pains. A wolf's right paw, tied around one's throat, was believed to ease the swelling caused by throat infections.

The gaze of a wolf was once thought to cause blindness.

Others believed that the breath of the wolf could cook meat.

Naturalists of the day believed wolves sharpened their teeth before hunting.

Dead wolves were buried at a village entrance to keep out other wolves. This belief is echoed today by farmers who continue to shoot predators and hang them on fence posts to repel other predators.

Travelers were warned about perils of walking through lonely stretches of woods, and stone shelters were built to protect them from attacks. Our modern word "loophole" is derived from the European term "loup hole," or wolf hole, a spy hole in shelters through which travelers could watch for wolves.

Spellbound by Animal Communications

Dinah Roseberry

Communicating with animals usually does not involve the casting of spells—though I've heard of many who would truly like to be able to turn someone (from time to time) into their animal of choice! Despite the little need of spells to strike up a conversation with the local animal kingdom, the very practice of talking with animals has that mystical allure that spell casting represents.

In past days, I'm sure that most folks have viewed animal communications as something that is difficult to perceive–and maybe even impossible to do. But that's not so. Many already have had a glimpse into the animal world merely by looking at their animals' daily behaviors and varied personality traits. Love allows that. Some of that trait noticing then infiltrates our busy minds and hides away deep in the recesses, next to the unwanted laundry list or the ceiling that needs painting in the back bedroom. Still, it's there and this is just the tip of the iceberg of what's hiding in the minds of animal lovers! And that's a good thing!

Naah, I hear you saying. *Oh, okay, yes, I can tell when my dog is hungry or when he's mad at me.* Or, *it's obvious to see that my cat has an attitude problem.*

But there's so much more to it than the mundane quirks that are visible to most who take the time to look. Moving these things aside for a moment, let's look even deeper. You've heard of this kind of communication certainly. Maybe you've even tried to send a message to your animal friends. Alas, if you fell flat on your face, it's not a big deal, and since no one knows that you're trying to send messages, well, what's the harm?!

The fact is, communicating with an animal is an easy thing to do and something that all pet people should learn. After all, you make every effort to talk and communicate with the other members of your family and household. Why, there may have even been a time, when a baby graced your presence and knew not what you were saying. Still, there was communication that oftentimes went beyond talking or body language. There is a knowing buried deep within all of us that allows us to communicate with those we care for.

Everyone Can and Should Talk to Animals

The most difficult part to perfecting this communication is one of non-acceptance. We as humans always doubt ourselves when it comes to things that are not scientifically based—this even if we are of the "spirited" type who are in touch with the mind/body/spirit world. We don't believe the messages we receive. Let us disperse this attitude and move forward.

To begin your trek down the animal communications lane, it becomes important for you to learn meditation. This is not a crazy zany way to call down the Gods. This is a way to quiet your mind so that you can hear messages, rather then the chatter that the brain pulls in from a variety of sources (including your own thoughts). For in the spaces between your chattering thoughts are the messages that can go and come in animal communications.

It's always easiest to find someone who will teach you, in a classroom environment, the ropes of this wonderful skill. Not only does it make the lessons go quickly, but it's a great deal of fun. (Money well spent.) Many are available now to teach and are as close as your Internet search engine. My personal classes came through an East Coast Communicator,

Anita Curtis (in Pennsylvania) who uses the Penelope Smith method. If a schoolroom is not to your liking, most animal communications books (including mine: *Psychic Pets, Solving Paranormal Mysteries*) have steps for you to take to become adept at talking to our furry friends.

When learning, there is usually a visualization exercise that teaches you who your animal guide is—we all have one—and your entire visualized scenario is born of this exercise. You will find your animal guide to be quite affectionate and willing to help you connect to the animal world. What I'm about to say is quite simplified and by no means a quick and easy guide to follow here, but basically, once you visualize your guide and the animal you want to talk with, you're on your way.

The trick, and often the deterrent, is that (just like other species) animals each communicate in different ways. Some are very intelligent, like my close personal friend, Bentley (Marla's cantankerous BIRD), and find our language perfectly easy to navigate. It's a matter of thinking thoughts, and certain animals (whether alive or deceased) can hear and respond clearly. Others, though, like my own now-deceased "Heinz 57" variety shelter DOG, Rufus, can only talk or understand in pictures. And thinking in pictures for me is none to easy at times. Too, if you have an animal that is obsessed about a particular thing (like the food!), communication can be clipped and sporadic.

Many communicate using a combination of techniques—just as we do during our days out in the world. The idea is to try a few different communication methods until you stumble upon the one, or ones, your animal responds to best. I suppose I should take a moment to tell you that for many, talking with your own animal can be more difficult than talking with someone else's. I liken this to the ease of telling a problem to someone on the outside of your family cluster rather than to someone on the inside, who is many times too busy to listen and too quick to judge. Even this, though, can be overcome by practice, practice, practice!

I'm often asked how it is possible that I'm talking with an animal, but the animal in question is busy in some other activity or even sleeping. This is where understanding the spirited world of love comes into play. When talking to an animal, you are communicating with the higher self spirit of that animal rather than the animal you may see sleeping on the floor. This is the spirit that is watching over all the lives of this one particular animal, much the same as your own higher self oversees all of your lives in the varied times, places, and dimensions. Maybe that's too much to digest at present, so suffice it to say that the animal will respond to you from another level of awareness—one that is not present or seen in the here and now. The fact is, the actual communication will become easier once you divorce yourself from the idea that the animal in front of you is communicating on your level. It is not.

I find it best to communicate with an animal that is not present. Then I don't have to fight that natural inclination to think that the animal is not acting the way an animal who is talking should. (However that is!)

Practice Makes Perfect

So let's try an exercise involving an animal that is not your own, but whom you know well enough. Choose an animal whose person is close enough to you to critique the outcome—that is, whether what you've picked up in your communication reflects the issues present for that animal at this time.

For this quick and easy trial, you won't need to find your animal guide (spirit knows you are experimenting and will compromise for this introductory phase). You will, however, need to find a quiet place where you can sit for a few moments in meditation, seeing in your mind's eye the animal you've chosen to talk with. Notice the nature of the animal. Look at the fur. Peer into the eyes. Touch it softly and see the movement of its breath.

When you feel you've relaxed enough and have visualized the animal, call out to it in a soft voice. Picture it looking up at you, tilting its head as if to listen to your question. Then picture the animal looking into its food bowl. The bowl is empty now and you see the animal note that and then look up to you. Ask in your mind:

What food would you like to see in your bowl if you could have anything you wanted?

Then quickly empty your mind and listen. Does a thought of a particular food pop into your mind? Or do you see the picture of a food? At this point, if you are relaxed and centered enough on the animal you've been watching, an answer should make its way to your brain. If you're watching a CAT, maybe you will see a canary in the bowl! A DOG might project a steak on the grill. A HORSE might give the vision a carrot dangling in front of him. Grasp the thought!

Now contact the person who owns the animal and discuss what you've seen. Most likely, you will find that the person will confirm for you the love the animal has for that certain food. Don't be surprised, too, if you see other things as well as food. Some things you see may not make sense, but you should make note of them anyway and tell the person what you've visualized no matter how strange it seems. Oftentimes, though it makes little sense to you, it makes perfect sense to the animal's owner.

A Job Well Done

Way before I'd ever tried animal communications, someone I'm very close to attempted an experiment on her own boisterous dog. Zippy was a GERMAN SHEPPARD with a mission. It was his job to find every dirty stick or rock possible and to then drop them on my friend's feet, scuffing her shoes, dirtying her pant legs, and often hurting her in the process. Zippy felt it was my friend's job to throw the stick or rock. Now. Again. And again. And the only way to force the issue was to drop it *on* her feet—every time, without fail.

My friend felt that there had to be a solution and she'd heard that animal communication was possible, though she wasn't entirely sure about it. But giving it a shot couldn't hurt. So she stood in front of Zippy and became very quiet, ignoring the stone that the DOG had dropped on her foot. She pictured in her mind Zippy picking up a big stick and laying it in *front* of her feet, rather than *on* them. She then pictured the same thing, only with a rock. After concentrating on this for several moments, she then reached down, picked up the stick and threw it.

Zippy dashed out after the stick! But this time when he came back, instead of depositing it on her feet, he stopped for a fraction of a second and then put the stick *in front of* her feet, looking up at her as though waiting for a " job well done" pat on the head. Animal communications worked!

A note to the wise, however: Things that involve behavior change (like Zippy's) will need reinforcing. As in any learning experience, repetition is an important part of learning. "If you don't use it, you lose it" is the thought to keep in mind. This goes for both your own ability to communicate with an animal or for the behavior you want changed to stay changed!

Start Simple

So start simple and believe in animal communications, and you will be able to accomplish a wondrous life with your pet! Just like all spell work, intention is the key to a virtuous success. That and love.

Your animal communications spell!

2 parts love
1 part desire
1 quieted mind

Mix well and offer to your animal of choice. Now think of the behavior you'd like to see changed or the message you'd like to send. Close your eyes and send the message.

Then speak the incantation.

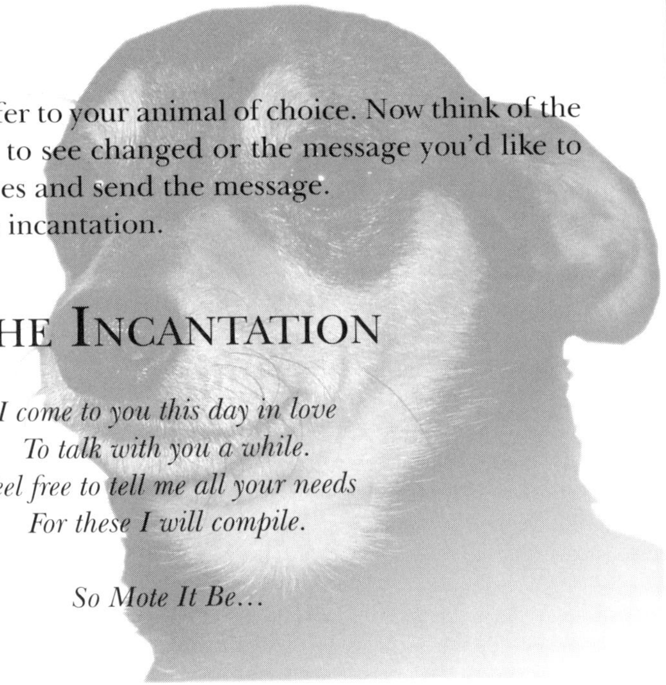

The Incantation

I come to you this day in love
To talk with you a while.
Feel free to tell me all your needs
For these I will compile.

So Mote It Be…

Healing Our Animal Friends With Energy

Reverend Tim Shaw

While often considered an alternative or holistic practice in our modern age, the use of energy healing is a modality that has been around for centuries. Before the advent of pharmaceuticals, shamans used energy to heal the maladies of both man and beast. These holy men would call upon the gods of old, through sacred rituals, to send the healing forces of nature down to the earth. Who among us has not prayed to a deity or an angel to intercede in order to bring balance or improve the health of a loved one?

In many cultures today, energy healing is not only accepted but is commonly practiced. Take the "laying on of hands" for instance. This type of healing utilizes many aspects of what we refer to as energy healing and is found to be acceptable by most major religions of the world.

When we discuss the use of energy in healing we need to understand just what it is. For our purposes, energy can be described as a form of vibration that makes up the world around us. We know from physics that everything is in a constant state of vibration. The slower something vibrates the easier it can be detected by our senses. Likewise, the quicker it vibrates, the harder it becomes for us to perceive it.

An example of vibrations that you cannot see, of course, are radio waves. They are invisible, yet we know that they exist each time we turn a radio on. Once we accept the fact that we are surrounded by a world of unseen vibrations, we may then begin to think about using them for healing purposes.

Who Can Benefit From Energy Healing?

All living beings can benefit from the use of energy, especially those little and not so little friends in our extended family. Animals are the perfect recipients of energy healing and are often very appreciative of it. Fortunately they have never been taught "societal imposed limitations" and are totally open to receiving energy. In fact, many animals will calm right down or fall asleep when receiving it.

The benefits of energetic healing can range from relieving pain to stimulating the immune system. Also those who channel this energy receive an added bonus. As the energy flows through them they in fact also receive a healing. Best of all anyone who has the desire can learn how to heal with energy in a relatively short amount of time.

The ABC's Of Simple Energy Healing

Belief

The very first aspect that needs to be addressed is your own belief system. Belief has absolutely nothing to do with religion. It is a state of mind in which you hold a premise to be true. What is important in energy healing is that you totally 100 percent believe what you are doing can and will work. Also, we must remember that belief is often described by many teachers as the "suspension of reality." Thus to be an effective Energy Healer, you must stop thinking that something is impossible or that you are somehow limited. You must believe that all concepts in this universe are possible. For only then will you have true belief.

Intentions

An intention is simply the reason why you are doing something. As a healer your intent is paramount and equally as important as belief when it comes to channeling healing energies. Never be afraid of intentions as we often use them several times a day when we say "I wish" or "I want." Believe it or not, it is quite similar to spell casting as your intent becomes a focused thought which acts as a beacon to effect whatever you wish accomplished. To further that notion, in the Spiritualist tradition there is an old adage that says, "Thoughts are Things." When you merely think about doing something, you have already put the gears of possibility and change into motion.

Meditation

I suggest that a short period of meditation, prayer, or quiet contemplation be done before any healing session is attempted. It is in this way that you will prepare your mind and body to become a channel for the healing energies that will flow through you. Always remember that a calm mind is the most effective tool in this type of work.

Focus

When working with any healing modality it is best to imagine that the individual to receive the energy healing, be it human or animal is the most important thing in your life at that moment. In this way the healing energies will flow through you and directly to who it is intended for.

Allowing The Energy To Flow

Visualize that a golden ribbon of energy is passing through the top of your head, your torso, down to your feet, back up your legs, and out your arms and hands. There are chakras or energy points located in the palms of your hands as well as your fingertips. It is these points that will project the energy out of your body and into the recipient's.

At first you may not feel anything different however after interviewing many fellow healers they agree that the more you work with energy, the more aware you will become of its presence. Oftentimes the healer may experience a tingling sensation in their body as it begins to flow. Also your palms may begin to become warm, sometimes even becoming flushed. These are common natural reactions to the energy flow.

Hand Movements

When working with animals, place one hand just below the inside neck where it meets the torso. With your other hand approximately 3 to 6 inches (where ever it feels right) from the animals head, slowly move it along the spine, working down to the haunches. As you pass your hands over certain areas, you may feel a slight "pull" or "tingling." If you should feel this, you may wish to keep your hands in that place until you feel appropriate to move or the feeling lessens.

Next, place your hand on the animals neck just above where it meets the spine. With your free hand slowly work down its shoulder to its front paws. Repeat this motion along the animals hips and back legs. If the animal is too large to actually reach that far, point the palm of your hand, fingertips up, at that region. The healing energy will flow to where it is intended.

Ending A Session

Energy seems to work on its own time and intensity. Once you have completed the suggested hand movements or feel the energy has begun to wane, it is time to close your session. With both hands open, touching, and with palms down, move them over the animals body from head to haunches 3 times saying

"With this I seal the healing that you have received."

You may wish to again keep your hands 3 to 6 inches off the animal.

Healing From Another Location

You may be surprised to know that you may send healing to anyone anywhere. All you need to do is enter into a meditative state and visualize whomever you wish to be the recipient of the healing in your mind. You may also use a photograph for better clarity. Visualize golden hue begin to surround them starting at the head and slowly descending to their hooves or paws. Let this imagery continue until you feel this energy begin to wane. When it does, say three times:

"With this I seal the healing that has been sent."

Healing Fish and Reptiles

Touching an animal or having it close to you is not always needed when healing animals such as reptiles and fish. Merely look at the animal that needs healing and follow the technique used when distance healing.

A Moment Of Thanks

After you end the session you should set aside some time to give thanks to whomever your deities are or to spend a few moments in quiet contemplation. Next, it is suggested that any negative energies that may have been removed from the animal be symbolically sent to the earth's molten core to be recycled back into positive energy. You may do this simply by making the intent of sending the negative energy away and shaking your hands in a downward motion.

The harnessing of the healing energy is one of the most fulfilling and rewarding things that you can do for a faithful friend. Just as we feed our animals a balanced diet and give them exercise, we can keep them healthy by working with the energies that are around us. They are, after all, more than pets; they are family.

Divination and Animals

Victoria Gross

On June 3, 2002, a new and innovated show called *Pet Psychic* aired on the Animal Planet channel, featuring British medium Sonya Fitzpatrick. The show ended on January 1, 2003. Each episode displayed Sonya's talents as she conversed with pet DOGS, CATS, and other species of the animal kingdom; thus opening the door to the recognition and acceptance of what we now call animal communication.

With trepidation, I had listed animal communication under services offered on my first flyer back in 1987. It was just starting to be talked about and I thought it would be cool to add it to my repertoire. Even though it sounded a little weird, (after all I am a Taurus), I kept it on the flyer with slight embarrassment. Some of my friends thought it was neat and I started reading their HORSES. My sister, Gloria, just shook her head though she had heard about HORSE owners using psychics to get to the root of problems they were having with their animals. So half joking and not sure if she believed it, she asked me to read for her horse Sadie. She was amazed when the information I gave proved to be accurate. To tell the truth, I was amazed. Shocked me right out of my gypsy shawl!

I always find it somewhat scary when reading animals. I mean, how does one really know they are communicating with the animal and not their own imagination. I guess the proof is in the paws or hoofs. I knew I was in trouble when someone came up to me at a psychic fair and asked if I would read their LIZARD. I took a deep breath and said the psychic next to me could do it, went home and removed the service of animal communication from the flyer. Now, I can't put it back on because it seems everyone is doing it, and I don't want to be a copycat—pardon the pun.

As I sit here writing this on my patio on a California summer night, my DOG, Buster, is communicating with another DOG through the air by barking. I wonder what they are saying. It is probably something to the effect, "I wish she would get off the dang computer and feed me" —yup, that's it alright. I am convinced that Buster is really an Ascended Master in a DOG's body with a Buddha belly and his challenge in life is to overcome slothfulness and gluttony.

All kidding aside, I do take the topic seriously and know that pet psychics have done a lot of good for both pets and their owners. Many have taken the advice that an authentic pet psychic has given and seen much improvement with their animals. That is where the proof lies. In the results.

Any psychic worth their salt will tell you that we rely on results to determine our accuracy. Of course, people have free will and can change the outcome of any reading, though with animals it is different. They do not have free will, so the results are vitally important.

As the Earth's energy changes and people are awakening to their natural sensitivities and animals have become more domesticated, it only makes sense that we can communicate with them on a telepathic level. In the book *Rosicrucian Cosmo-Conception* by Max Heindal, he states that "...animals are governed by a group-spirit. This group-spirit governs the actions of animals as they do not have the faculty of self-consciousness..." I believe that as humans evolve, the group-spirit also evolves. The more the animals are domesticated, the more their energy fields integrate with human owners and they rise to the astral level of feelings. That is why it is easier to read domesticated animals over animals in the wild. Don't get me wrong, we can communicate with wild animals; I've told a wild coyote and a couple of young deer to stay away from the road. They come out of the foothills when it is hot looking for food and water. After a warning for their safety, they have retreated.

Buster, Victoria's dog now resides on the otherside.

So it can be done with wild animals, though I am not sure that they can communicate back to us due to their evolution. Any DOG owner will tell you, the longer they have the DOG, the more human it becomes. Depending on the evolution of a particular species determines the psychic connection available.

Now, what does all of this have to do with divination? Well, the way I see it, it behooves us to understand the psychic make up of the animal kingdom as that can give us deeper clarity when working with animals as guides and totems.

Today, there are a myriad of animal Tarot and oracle cards out on the market ranging from the beautiful and meaningful to the downright silly. In 1989, I received my first deck of animal cards as a Christmas present from my dear friend and mentor now living in the spirit world, Barbara Ramondino. Brand new out on the market, the *Medicine Cards* by Jamie Sams and David Carson, were published in 1988 by Bear and Company and to my knowledge may be the first animal cards to hit the market. September 9, 1995, I attended a book signing at a metaphysical bookstore called *Visions and Dreams*, located in Costa Mesa, California, and had the great pleasure of meeting Ted Andrews, author of *Animal Speak*. Like the cards, the magic of working with animal totems swirled around me as if casting a spell. Twenty years later, I still have those cards. Worn and tattered, they are my treasure. I have the book sitting next to me on the table, highlighted and earmarked pages reveal secrets that animals can and will tell us if we just take time to listen.

My favorite deck to pull a daily card from is Steven Farmer's *Power Oracle Cards*. I pulled a card, read the meaning then went to the *Animal Speak* book for deeper clarification. The card I drew for the day I wrote this chapter was SEAL, with the keyword "Imagination."

Well now, if that wasn't appropriate, I didn't know what was. Turning to the *Animal Speak* book, I checked out to see what Ted Andrews said about the SEAL as an animal totem. His key words were:

> ...active imagination, creativity and lucid dreaming...

He went on to say,

> When the SEAL shows up in our life as a totem, it is time to ask ourselves some questions. Questions such as: Are you getting out of balance? Has the imagination faculty opened so much that you are

not staying grounded? Are you listening to things and people that you shouldn't? Are you not listening to that which you should?

We all know that SEALS spend a lot of time in water, so the element of water plays a significant role in further determining the message that SEAL brings us. The author goes on to say,

> Water is the creative element. It is a symbol of the feminine, the emotional, the imaginative, and the dreamtime...

Another aspect that I find interesting when reading this, is the fact that SEALS come out of the water to rest and to mate. This symbolism is extremely valuable as it shows us the importance of staying balanced. We can't spend all our time in the etheric world; if we do, nothing can manifest on the physical plane. In other words, we do the work on the invisible plane, then remove our attention from it so that it can develop and come into fruition. If you keep working on something over and over, chances are it won't manifest. It's like watering a plant too much. Over saturation will drown the plant. Same premise with the imagination. Mr. Andrews final words on the chapter on SEALS states,

> The archetypal force of the SEALS and SEA LIONS helps those with them as totems to learn to balance the inner imagination with the outer realities-making both aspects more colorful and beneficial...

Wow, what a great totem for the day, energies I can focus on.

In the mid-nineties, I co-owned a metaphysical bookstore for a little while in Fullerton, California. My business partner, Sherry Williams, originally owned the store which was called *The Enchanted Spirit.* I had a small business which I named *The Crescent Moon* and we decided to join our efforts and talents together. Sherry is a gifted energy worker, and one day when I was having an energy session with her, a LYNX jumped right into my body. I saw the animal standing next to the table I was laying on and after I acknowledged her, she jumped on top of me and her essence permeated my whole being and she has been with me ever since.

Lynx stand for *Secrets and Visions of the Hidden and Unseen.* Now, some people say that you shouldn't tell others who your animal totems are, that it takes away from their power. I don't prescribe to that way of thinking as I don't think anything or anyone but ourselves can diminish the power of our animal totems, and the only way we do that is by not using them. It has been my experience that they are always with us. Even when I have left the power dormant for a while, when I call upon her, she is always ready to spring into action. Another time, when I was going through a low and rough period of my life, the Black Panther came to assist me through many a dark days. The keywords for that animal is "*Reclaiming One's True Power.*" The right animal always comes to me when needed. They know who we are and what we need.

When working with the *Medicine Cards,* I like to choose the *Pathway Spread* to give me clarity on what is going on in my life, or with a particular situation. On page twenty-seven and twenty-eight in the book which accompanies the cards, you will find the layout meanings and diagram of the *Pathway Spread*.

Positions:

Card 1: Your Past

Card 2: Your Present

Card 3: Your Future

Card 4: The Pattern or set of life lessons that is moving through your life now

Card 5: The Challenge you have conquered or the lesson just competed

Card 6: What is working for you

Card 7: What is working against you

Now let's take a look at the cards I've drawn — or I should say the cards that drew me, as before I ever draw any animal cards, I always ask that the right animal(s) come to me with the message needed.

These are the cards:

Card 1: Porcupine – Innocence and Trust

Card 2: Mountain Lion – Leadership

Card 3: Eagle – Spirit

Card 4: Squirrel – Gathering

Card 5: Skunk – Reputation – Walk Your Talk
Card 6: Buffalo – Prayer and Abundance
Card 7: Turtle – Mother Earth – Cleansing

So you see, we put the meanings of the cards and the meanings of the placements together to give us deeper insight to what is going on. In card position 1 through 6, read the regular message, with card 7, you will read the Contrary message. I do say, the perfect animals came to me on that day as always. I take heart at the gifts they offer.

Again, there are many different animal decks that are available to use. As with the Tarot, you need to find the deck that speaks to you, one that you are comfortable with. Working with animal totems has surely enriched my life through good times and bad. My hope is that you will find the same wisdom, comfort and feeling of connectedness as I have. Enjoy the beauty and pay attention to the magick of the animals as they come in to bless your life.

Animal Amulets

An amulet or talisman is an ornament or piece of jewelry thought to give protection from evil, danger or disease. They come in all shapes and sizes, and each has it's own meaning and special power.

Humans have been wearing amulets for thousands of years. Gemstones and crystals have long been known to bring positive emotional and physical healing results to both humans and animals.

In addition to mainstream Western medicine, one of the alternative healing treatments for pets includes the use of crystals, gemstones, and minerals from the earth. Many pet owners have discovered that by attaching a gemstone and crystal amulet to the animal's collar, the gemstones brought about a faster recovery. Gemstones and crystals contain natural healing powers that work just by having the animal, or human, wear the stones next to their skin.

Here is a listing of the various commonly used animal shaped amulets that are used to protect and heal our pets.

ALLIGATOR TEETH

Worn to protect against all forms of sorcery, power to heal the body and counteract poison.

BADGER

Gives the wearer the power and willingness to fight for what they want by whatever means possible, even the unconventional.

BAT

Asian charm depicts five BATS as the blessing of health, wealth, love of virtue, old age, and a natural death. It also protects the wearer from hexes, enemies, and all forms of black magick.

BEAR

Childbearing, powerfully protective mother instincts, hibernation; symbolizes introspection and self-renewal.

BEAVER

The *builder*, not only of one's home but also, symbolically, of one's career *and* one's relationships (starting with oneself).

BEES, BEETLES, WINGED INSECTS

Harbingers of Sprint, Earth's fertility, social cooperation, industriousness.

BULL

Increases fertility in women and virility in men.

BUTTERFLY

Ancient symbol of the soul, exemplifies transformation; represents an early and happy marriage in some Asian cultures.

CAT

Personal pride, self-assurance, love of beauty, comfort, and good luck.

COUGAR

Leadership.

COW

Earth mother, nourishment, taking care of physical needs, the wealth of the Earth, fertility cycles of the Moon.

COYOTE

Cleverness, guise of the trickster, surviving by ones wits.

CRAB

To increase fertility and bring love into your life.

DEER

Maternal affection, healing touch, grace, gentility and fertility.

DOG

Companionship, fidelity, household guardian. Keeps all malicious persons and evil spirits from entering your home.

DOLPHIN

Protects against accidents when traveling by ship.

DONKEY

Brings extra good luck.

DOVE

Brings peace into the home and workplace.

DRAGON

Love, happiness, fertility, dispels negative vibrations and bad luck.

DRAGONFLY

Ethereal, illusionary beauty.

ELK'S TOOTH

Dispels negativity and brings good fortune.

FISH

Fertility, virility, and prosperity. Protection from people with evil intentions.

FOX

Adaptability, cunning, prosperity.

FROG

Transformation, evolution, small impulses that lead to meaningful things; also, the herald of nourishing rain and the beginning of spring. Helps to promote friendship and reconcile enemies.

HORSE

Great power coupled with great gentility, personal power in both physical and spiritual domains.

LADYBUG

Good luck coming from the gifts of the Love Goddess.

LAMB

Innocence, the playful vitality of youth. Increases fertility and fills the home with peace.

LION

Courage, boldness, and nobility. Protects against danger while traveling, helps overcome enemies and strengthens emotions.

LIZARD

Basking habits show the LIZARDS' love of the Sun, and the Sun returns that love; symbolized the solar powers that value and nourish even the small things.

MOLE

Gives the power to skillfully move and explore below the surface of things.

MOUSE

The importance of the small things in life.

PIG

Their rounded shape suggests pregnancy, fertility, and abundance, their rooting around also associates them with the Earth mysteries.

RABBIT

Fertility, sexuality, abundance.

RAM

Fertility.

SCARAB BEETLE

Transformation, rebirth into eternal life. Wear for good luck and protection against all evil forces.

SERPENT

Associated with the healing arts because of self-renewal and spiraling coils suggesting the flow of the life Force; and going into the ground represents knowledge of the mysteries.

SHARK

Worn for strength and control.

SNAKE

Worn for wisdom and to increase sexual power.

SPIDER

The web of life (ancient symbol relevant to modern ecology), personal skill, good luck for craft persons and witches.

TIGER

Physical strength and immortality.

TOAD

A spirit of place that confers well being to a home; recognizing beauty in homely things.

TURTLE

Longevity and protective security; strengthening of divinatory power.

UNICORN

Purity, innocence, justice, fertility, and sexual magnetism.

WOLF

Finding new energy by making contact with the inner, wild, and primitive level of being.

Birds

BIRDS (GENERAL)

Thought, imagination, intuition, freedom.

BIRDS (WATER)

Associated with abundance, fertility, and transformation.

CHICKEN

Security and prosperity of a cozy homestead.

DOVE

Peace, love, and fertility.

EAGLE

Spiritual power, the ability to soar beyond all limitations. Protects people and structures against lightning.

HAWKS

Alertness, awareness, ability to see the heart of the matter.

OWL

Wisdom, knowledge, go-betweens twixt night and day, life and death, the Middle Earth and the Underworld.

PARROT

A love for exotic places, communication, and sociability.

PEACOCK

Personal pride, love of beauty, and immortality.

PHEASANT

For safety and protection while traveling by air.

ROOSTER

Courage; the victory of light over dark.

SEA GULL

Ability to travel through many dimensions as gulls are at home in three elements: Earth, Air, Water. An appropriate symbol for the Shaman.

STORK

Believed to bring babies because it is an ancient symbol of incipient life. Symbolizes good parenting and a reciprocal devotion to ones own parents.

SWALLOW

Attracts good luck, keeps the home safe from evil sorcery, ghosts, fire, and lightning.

SWAN

Feminine grace and beauty that stirs Divine inspiration.

Animal Totems

Willie Windwalker Gibson

People think the only spirits are the human ones. In fact, animals are spirits too, and they come back to help and guide us.

Just because an animal gets old, sick, or has a mishap that causes them to cross over, doesn't mean they still can't communicate with us. I have had many cases where a client will say that they felt their CAT or DOG sitting besides them on the bed. I tell them that they came back to say hello and let them know that they are with them always.

Animal spirits are also our guardian angels that warn us of danger. I have had people tell me that they had felt a tug just before they've stepped off a curb in front of an oncoming car, stopping them from being run over and the tug was felt on the pant leg or skirt about the height of a DOG or CAT.

Native American cultures revere certain animals as special as well. The WOLF is a creature that is considered to be a very spiritual animal. It is a wise teacher and cunning problem solver. The EAGLE is a BIRD that represents God or the great spirit. Yes, different animals represents different things and messages.

I do animal totem readings with cards. The cards have different pictures on them that when dealt in a certain sequences tell a story.

Through these cards, I tell what I see to the client. The client uses the information to see what is going on in his or her life at that point in time, and for future events.

For instance, if I spread out a series of five cards say, a TURTLE, an EAGLE, a DOLPHIN, a HAWK, and SNAKE, that could mean that the great spirit sends a message that this person needs spiritual balance in his or her life.

The animal totems give me a source of information and a path to follow. Whether or not the client follows what the animal totems say is up to them. You would be surprised at how many people don't. I tell them that they have free will to do what they want, even if it's the wrong thing to do. Clients will also ask me to ask the totems for a winning lottery ticket. I tell them the readings don't work that way. If they did, I would be a millionaire instead of being behind on my mortgage!

In order for a animal totem reading to be effective, you have to believe that the animal totem spirits can help you. This doesn't mean to not believe in whatever religion you follow. I am a firm believer that a person has a right to believe in any religion they want. I believe in the great spirit (God). Yes, I am a Shaman but am also a Christian Minister. I use my faith daily walking both paths. It serves me well also when I read the animal totems. Animals are God's creatures and they serve him also. That's why many of my clients like the animal totems instead of regular Tarot decks. The unique pictures and spreads I use captivates the person I am reading for. It offers them a different read, and there are not many who read the animal totems.

I also use animal totems when I do clearings for people and property. Just before I go out on such a case I conduct a reading, giving me some idea of what I am up against. Using the direction of the great spirit through animal totems has helped me with many cases.

One case involved a cold murder case in which I was asked by the victim's family to look into the murder of their daughter. I was sent pictures of the victim and a piece of her jewelry. I looked at the items but I was being blocked for some reason.

I took out my animal totem deck and shuffled seven cards. The way the cards fell told me that the murderer was a family friend. I relayed the message to the family. They wrote me back and told me that they had thought the same thing.

The information was passed on to police and the case was solved. I didn't get credit for the information. That was okay as long as the murderer was caught, and once again, the animal totems gave me a path to follow for an answer.

Many call this fortune telling, and that's okay. I know it works for me and that the great spirit uses the totems to tell me things to help people.

The energy of the animal totems is used for the greater good always. They are not used to hurt people. Animal totems are read by only the gifted few. The cards have to become a part of the reader, like a third arm. If the cards don't feel right to a person, then the totems are not meant for them to read.

The best thing I can tell people is to find a medium that feels right to them. If you're a reader, find a deck that fits you. If not a deck, then perhaps runes or crystals. There will be something out there that fits your psychic energies.

Choosing the Right Pet Through Astrology

Some people choose their pets, and others are chosen by them. Two out of my three found us.

Bentley the Cockatiel was given to me as a gift. I had no idea about the care and feeding of birds at the time, and he, being a hatchling, was pretty suspicious about me as well. Fortunately, we managed to overcome our doubts about each other, and 25 years later, we were still on speaking terms, so I've taken that as a positive!

Pipsqueak the cat was born to a feral mother under my house. I always feed the strays, and knew that Pipsqueak was the runt of the litter. One stormy morning when she was about 6 weeks old, I guess she decided to defect because I opened the back door and there she was, sitting out in the rain, looking like a little drenched rat, mewing to come in. Needless to say, she's been a pampered house cat ever since.

In the case of Kalli the dog, we did the finding… at a local animal shelter when she was just a few weeks old. She now rules the roost, so to speak, or at least thinks she does until she, a 100 pound dog, gets anywhere near tiny little Pipsqueak. One hiss from the cat and Kalli turns tail and runs in the other direction.

I kind of like the idea that pets will find us, and firmly believe that they do for a reason, so I'm perfectly happy to welcome a pet into our home despite their birth signs, but some people prefer to choose their pets very carefully and that lead me to wonder if, when choosing a pet, their birth signs made any difference as to their temperament, so I asked my friend, astrologer David Wells, if the same Zodiac traits that we humans have apply to animals as well, and he said they do. So if you're looking to choose a pet according to their birth sign, or just curious to see whether your pet fits his/her astrological profile, here is some basic information about each sign, their personality traits, and maybe some insight into why they do the things they do.

Aries – March 21-April 20:

An Aries pet is bold and adventurous and will be fiercely independent and not very good at taking orders from others. They have a tendency to brood when asked to do something they do not want to do. They can also be a bit self-centered and are easily spoiled. These pets will be the leaders of the others in your household and will be extremely territorial.

Taurus –April 21-May 21:

Those born under the sign of Taurus are deeply sensitive and quite stubborn at times, but are not difficult to train. They have a placid nature and also have the tendency to be a bit lazy. If spoiled and surrounded by "creature comforts," they will absolutely wallow in it. They are quite loyal.

Gemini – May 22-June 21:

GEMINI pets react quickly to situations, and try to take everything in all at once, which is probably good, but at the same time, this makes them a bit on the nervous side and they seem to be constantly wound up. They definitely have lots of energy to spare. They are very intelligent, are big show offs and therefore love to learn new tricks so that they can perform.

Cancer – June 22-July 22:

If your pet is born under the sign of the CRAB, you'll find them to be very complex creatures. They are fragile nurturers, both unpredictable and temperamental and need constant support and encouragement. These animals need to be needed, are easily offended and are prone to sulk and wallow in self pity for a long time when they get their feelings hurt. They are also the embodiment of the phrase "giving unconditional love," and truly see themselves as your child.

Leo – July 23-August 21:

LEO pets will keep you on your toes. They are born leaders, love new experiences and despise regular routines. If these pets get bored, they will create their own drama. They are very proud animals, sometimes to the point of appearing arrogant but at the same time are very friendly and outgoing. They need to be admired and never ignored. They are pretty fearless, except when it comes to cats.

Virgo – August 22-September 23:

A VIRGO animal is a very clean, fastidious animal and will not tolerate sloppy surroundings. It is said they are the cleanest animals of all the signs. They prefer working to playing and are quite vocal at mealtime. They need time to analyze all the facts about situations so people sometimes get the impression that they are indecisive or slow-witted, which is not the case. They are deep thinkers.

Libra – September 24-October 23:

Animals born under the sign of LIBRA have very soulful eyes and communicate well through them. They also possess excellent instincts and intuition and generally have a very easygoing attitude. These pets demand respect and under certain circumstances will appear to be quite courageous. They are bit indecisive, can be very stubborn, but are affectionate and for the most part enjoy the company of other animals in the house.

Scorpio – October 24-November 22:

SCORPIOS are quite persistent and determined. They will work hard for what they want and never give up. At the same time, they are very adaptable and versatile creatures but also fierce competitors with an excellent memory. Their loyalty knows no bounds and they can be very entertaining at times.

Sagittarius – November 23-December 22:

Animals born under the sign of SAGITTARIUS are not moody at all and sometimes it can seem like they are emotionally detached. They do get irritable when they are bored, however. They are fun-loving creatures, and can be considered the class clowns of the zodiac but with that comes the tendency to be a bit accident prone.

Capricorn – December 23-January 20:

CAPRICORNS might seem melancholy and boring at first because they evaluate everything and they don't take unnecessary chances. These are very self-sufficient animals but also need a structured way of life to feel safe and secure. They hate to be alone. They usually act older than their true age. Even as puppies and kittens, they seem to be wise beyond their years.

Aquarius – January 21-February 19:

These pets tend to be rebels just for the sake of having their own way, but are otherwise very gentle creatures. They will continue to do something their way to the point of stubbornness. Their two greatest loves are water and food, so bath time will be easy, but you'll have to keep an eye on their food intake and not leave tempting morsels unattended. These creatures need lots of freedom, and don't generally like being tethered.

Pisces – February 20-March 20:

The Pisces pet is very mysterious and elusive. They are molded by their surroundings. These animals are extremely compassionate and very sensitive to their owners' moods. If something is wrong, they are deeply affected. They are creatures of habit and not crazy about change and usually attach themselves deeply to one particular human in the house.

Setting Up an Animal Altar and Dedication Ritual

An altar is a sacred space upon which offerings are made for a variety of reasons. They are used particularly in the religions of Buddhism, Hinduism, Shinto, Taoism, as well as Christianity, Thelema, Neopaganism, and in Ceremonial magick.

Any surface can be used, although some traditions prefer a particular type of wood, stone, or other natural material. The altar may be of any shape and size, or even a patch of ground.

The items brought to the altar may be a random assortment of personally significant items or a particular set of items with ritual significance.

What you put on your pet altar is a personal choice. If you have more than one pet, you might want to make it a multi-purpose altar to include them all.

Traditionally, altar items may include candles of significant colors, cups or bowls or cauldrons, small statues of gods and goddesses, a ritual knife, a wand, a bowl of salt, a bell, and possibly some crystals. The altar is usually covered in some sort of cloth. Some traditions separate the items on the altar into the four Greek classical elements, of earth, air, fire, and water; other traditions assign gender preferences to the items and believe they signify the masculine/feminine principles.

In addition to my regular pet altar, we also have a small, separate memorial altar in the house that includes the ashes of our previous pets along with a favorite toy of each and their pictures.

To consecrate and dedicate an altar first find the place where you wish to set it up. This place must not be disturbed, for it will take on sacred and holy energies, and you will not want anything to happen to this area.

Use some quiet meditational music as you build your altar and remember, the more energy and work that you put into it, the more magickal energy it will take on. You can even use an energy bell or Tibetan singing bowl at the start to call upon your spirit guides to assist you with your work and to raise energy.

Once you have found that place, take a smudge wand of Sage, light it and begin to clear the air around the altar. Keep Love and Light in your consciousness throughout the process. Now, move to the four elements and ask for their guiding presence.

North =Earth
South = Fire
East = Air
West = Water
All Around = Spirit

Ask for their blessings and honor their assistance. Next, begin to set up the altar, placing each item you wish on the altar gently and reverently.

Once your altar is set up the way you want it, spend a few moments in quiet meditation thinking about what this altar means to you. Then allow the altar to fill you with its magick and energy. Feel the magick around you. Breathe in the Love and Light.

When you are done, sound the bell once again, thanking all elements and guides for their presence and assistance. Send them back harming none on their way. Now, thank the Lord and Lady for their presence in your life. Take a deep breath of the fresh magick around you and repeat:

So Mote It Be! It Is Done!

Deities for Animal Spell Work

These are a few of the renowned animal protector deities. Call upon them during your spell work as needed.

Spirits That Protect Animals in General:
Aphrodite, Artemis, Hathor, Lilith, Faunus

Spirits That Protect Cats:
Artemis, Bastet, Freya, Hecate, Lilith

Spirits That Protect Dogs:
Artemis, Hecate, Ogun, Saint Roch

Spirits That Protect Horses:
Anat, Demeter, Epona, Poseidon, Rhiannon

Spirits that Protect Toads:
Agwe, Heket

Spirits That Protect Snakes:
Athena, Lillith, Ezili, Simbi, Dahomey

Spirits That Protect Cows:
Brigid, Hathor, Hermes, Isis, Shiva

Spirits that Protect Fish:
Atargatis, Yemaya

Spirits That Protect Pigs:
Demeter, Seth

Animal Spells

What is offered here are a group of spells covering many needs. You may use them as they are, or as a guideline to create your own spells depending on your particular needs.

As I've often said, spells that we create ourselves are the most powerful because of our emotions during their creation. That's not to say that the following spells will not be effective. I will never put a spell in a book that has not been tried first, but remember, it's what you, the spell caster, puts *into* a spell that determines what you get out of it.

Whether you create your own spell or use the ones I have made, you might want to keep a magickal journal or make notes in your *Book of Shadows* during the spell construction phase, and then keep track of results as they begin to manifest.

It has been said that if a spell does not work out within a Lunar Month, you may want to rethink it and rework it by deciding what parts of the spell need to be changed.

Animal Candle Protection Spell

Animals, just like the rest of us have many things to be wary of. Predators, illness, and remaining safe in general. This is an all-purpose spell to keep them out of harms way.

> You will need:
>
> 1 brown candle
> Lotus, Bayberry or Violet incense
> Myrrh oil

If you can find a brown candle in the likeness of your pet, so much the better. If not, a regular brown candle will do.

Have your pet with you as you do this spell. Light the incense, anoint the candle with Myrrh oil; then close your eyes and picture in your mind a circle of bright white light around you and your pet. This is a protective light. Then repeat the following incantation:

Child of the Earth and child of my own,
Danger to you I will not condone.
May this protective light never wane
And free from harm you will remain.

So Mote it Be

Let the candle burn as you meditate on the incantation. When you feel that your message has been sent, blow out the candle, rub the smoke in the palms of your hands, then open your palms upwards and release your message into the ethers.

Healthy Pet Parchment Spell

There are times that our pets need the care of a veterinarian, and regular check-ups are mandatory to help insure their well-being, but spell work can also aid in keeping your little loved ones happy and healthy, and this spell is designed to do just that.

You will need:

1 small piece of parchment paper
A pen with blue ink
Carnation or rose geranium oil
A blue candle
A small cauldron or flameproof bowl

Anoint the candle with the oil, then light the candle and write down the following request on the parchment:

I call upon Aphrodite, Artemis, Hathor, Lilith and Faunus, protectors of all creatures great and small.

Watch over (pet name) and keep him/her in the best of health and out of harm's way.

May his/her body and soul be rendered healthy under your protection, guidance and good grace.

So Mote it Be

Concentrate on your intention for a moment or two, then light the parchment with the candle flame and drop it into the cauldron or flameproof bowl. As it burns, repeat the following incantation:

By the power of flame and the heat of fire
Please do my bidding for the task I require

So Mote It Be

Watch to make sure the parchment is completely burned before you walk away.

Blowing Away Bad Habits

Whether it's peeing in the house, excessive barking, or your kitty scratching up your furniture, our pets sometimes need a little bit of help to control or break a bad habit or two.

> You will need:
>
> 1 dandelion that is at its "fluff" stage
> White jasmine incense

Go out into your yard or to a neighborhood park to find yourself a dandelion. Pick the dandelion, thanking Flora, the Goddess of Nature, for her offering. Be careful not to knock off the fluff. Then find a quiet spot to sit.

Light the incense, hold the flower in front of you, concentrate on the bad habit that you'd like to see your pet stop and repeat the following incantation:

A deep breath in, a strong breath out
This habit (pet's name) can do without.
As I blow the fluff into the air
I send with it a healing prayer.
May this bad habit be withdrawn
And all memory of it be forever gone.

So Mote It Be

Hold the flower close to your mouth and blow off the fluff. As you watch it scatter and fly away, envision the bad habit flying away with it.

To Find A Lost Pet

For this spell you'll need to call upon a tree that is preferably in your yard or very near your home.

You will need:
One of your pet's favorite toys A small dish of their favorite food A bowl of water A tree fertilizer spike

Take all of the above to the tree. Tell the tree that your pet has gone missing and that you are very concerned. Ask the tree to provide a beacon for your pet to follow to find its way home, then repeat the following incantation:

My wayward child, look to this tree.
It's branches are for you to see.
It will guide you back to me.
Please come home soon.

So Mote It Be

Leave the toy and the food next to the tree and then plant the fertilizer spike at the eastern-most base of the tree as an offering of thanks for its assistance.

Check the tree often and put fresh food and water out every day.

Calming Your Pet

Anyone who owns a pet knows that they, like us, have times when they are stressed out and need a little bit of assistance in calming themselves down.

When my "kids" get stressed from time to time, I usually sit down, pet their heads, make eye contact, and talk quietly to them, and at the same time, I place my pentacle on them so that they can draw some of my positive energy from it. Magickal stones or crystals work the same way.

You will need:

An aquamarine, lace agate, rhodonite, or moonstone

First consecrate the stone with sea salt or moonlight, then take the stone into your hand and pour your healing energy into it.

As you talk to your pet, rub the stone over them while you pet them and repeat the following incantation:

Anxiety, fear, and unrest begone.
All negativity must be withdrawn.
A sense of calm and all around wellbeing
Will be brought on by this stone as it generates healing.

So Mote It Be

Repeat as often as necessary.

Protecting Pets From Negative Spirits

As you well know, animals are a great deal more sensitive to spirits, both good and bad, than many humans. There are various ways to keep them safe; some are exactly the same as what we do to protect ourselves, such as surrounding them with white light, but there are a few extra things that we can do for them in the house as well. One of the simplest is an image protection spell.

You will need:

A photograph of your pet
Protection Oil

On the photo, draw the image of a pentagram, protective rune, sigil, or any other symbol of your choosing.

As you look at the photo, envision your pet surrounded by bright, impenetrable white light. With that in mind, anoint the photo with Protection Oil and place it on your pet's altar. If you haven't made them an altar of their own, then keep it on yours.

Remember to touch up the oil every few days and refresh the white light on a daily basis.

You can purchase Protection Oil, or make your own. Here are two recipes:

Recipe One

4 drops Basil
3 drops Geranium
2 drops of pine
1 drop of Vetivert

~~~~~~~~~~~~~~~~~~~~~~~~~~~~~~~~

Recipe Two

1 dram Patchouli
1 dram Frankincense
1 dram Myrrh
1 tsp. Broken Mandrake
3 heaping teaspoons of sea salt
~~~~~~~~~~~~~~~~~~~~~~~~~~~~~~~~

Healing a Pet

While conventional veterinary care is best when dealing with a sick or injured animal, once the animal has been treated, you can help boost the healing process with this simple spell.

> You will need:
>
> 1 white candle
> Amber, carnation, or Myrrh incense

Light the candle and incense; then find a comfortable spot for you both of you to be together. Sit next to your pet and envision a circle of white light placed around the two of you. Then pray for a circle of blue light to be placed around you both for healing.

With this in place, repeat the following prayer:

Artemis, Goddess of Light And Protector of the
Vulnerable, give strength and healing to (pet's name)
during this time of infirmity. Bless him/her with
a quick recovery and continued good health.
So Mote It Be.

Let the candle and incense burn out on their own.

Animal Protection Charm Bag

Charm bags hold all the ingredients of a spell together in one place, which not only keeps the energy strong, but also keeps it flowing out into the ethers. This particular charm bag is created to help keep your pet safe.

You will need:

A piece of purple velvet that you can form into a bag
A coin that was minted in the animal's birth year
A Tiger's Eye crystal or Scarab
A sprig of sage or marjoram
A bay leaf
A stick of Myrrh incense

Cut the material into two squares of equal length and width. Arrange your material so that it makes a pouch; then sew the bottom and sides of your pouch together.

Fill the bag with coin, crystals, herbs, and incense.

As you sew the opening of your bag closed, repeat the following incantation:

Crystals, coins, herbs, and scent
Keep this child from discontent
Protection is the key word here
Let him/her live free of danger
And fearfulness be a stranger

So Mote It Be

Sew a ribbon on your bag and either hang it up by the ribbon, or place it on your altar, your pet's altar, or in a safe location.

Keeping Pets Safe From Malevolent Magick

It's sad but true. Sometimes bad magick is aimed at animals in order to hurt the owner. Perhaps a farmer is doing well, yet his neighbor is having a bad run of luck. Or maybe you have had conflict with a neighbor who decides to take it out on your dog in the non-physical sense.

Whatever the case, the simplest way to keep your pets or livestock out of harm's way is to:

- Hang bunches of mugwort on your fences, gates, or around the perimeter of your property. This will keep them safe from malevolent magick and spiritual danger. Also, horseshoes work as well on pets as they do on humans, so it's a good idea to hang one, or a small horseshoe amulet on the dog house, the birds cage, your aquarium, or the kitty's favorite sleeping spot.

- In ancient times, a whole raw egg was rubbed on the animal working from head to tail then down. After that, the egg was taken outside the house and disposed of.

- A red clover protective bath was also used. An infusion was created by pouring boiling water over red clover. The solids were strained out and the liquid was used to bathe the animals to keep them protected, healthy and thriving.

New Pet Blessing

It's always a wonderful thing to bring a new pet into your life, and it is our goal to keep them safe, healthy and happy.

The type of pet you invite into your family will determine which deity you call upon to assist with this blessing, so here is the short list:

Diana	for dogs
Bast	for cats
Melusine	for fish
Rhiannon	for birds
Athena	for turtles
Rhea	for rodents
Medusa	for snakes

You will need:

A rose quartz crystal
A simple gold ring or hoop
A sprig of marjoram
A blue candle
A sharp pin
Myrrh oil
A small velvet pouch
Tibetan singing bowl (optional)

Since it may be difficult for you to do this blessing with your new pet present (puppies and kittens may not sit still) you can use a picture or effigy of the new pet instead.

If you happen to have a singing bowl, you can use it to raise energy before you start your spell.

Place the picture of your pet in front of you; then etch his/her name into the candle, anoint the candle with Myrrh oil and then light it.

Take the rose quartz crystal into your hand and say:

With an open heart and
unconditional love,
I welcome you into my life.

Then pick up the ring and say:

This ring symbolizes eternity.
May our souls never be parted.

Take the marjoram and wrap it around both the ring and crystal and say:

You are my child and I promise
you love and protection
forever and always.

So Mote it Be.

Place the picture, the ring, the rose quartz, and the marjoram in the pouch and tuck it away in a safe place where it will not be disturbed.

New Pet Blessing II

Sometimes when you get a new pet, it takes a little while to bond and for them to feel comfortable in their new environment. They are usually nervous about new surroundings and we are nervous that we're not doing enough to make them feel at home. This blessing will work wonders for both of you.

You will need:

1 white candle
1 stick of gardenia or rose incense
1 sharp pin

Etch a heart in the candle with the pin and write your name and your pet's name or initials inside the heart.

Light the candle and the incense and with your pet in your arms, recite the following incantation:

Rub the belly, pat the head
Make sure that you're always fed
Hold you close three times a day
That will take your fear away
Romp and play, a life carefree
Forever it will always be
Blessings upon you, little one
May your life be filled with sun

So Mote It Be

Blow out the candle and let the incense burn itself out unless you will be leaving the house.

Happy Family Spell

When you have more than one pet, especially if they are of different types, not everyone is going to get along with the other. In order to help insure bliss rather than bluster, you might want to try this spell.

You will need:

Small bits of hair from each pet
A green leaf from your favorite tree
One strand of your hair

Collect the hair from your pets. Just giving them a quick brush should be all the hair you need.

Mix their hair together and then roll it up in the leaf, rolling towards you.

Fasten it with a strand of your own hair and repeat the following incantation:

Just a small pinch of each of your hair
Bound neatly together will stave off warfare
With my hair to bind you with love all around
There will be no more of the old battleground
Peace and harmony is the order of the day
And all bad feelings will be buried away

So Mote it Be

Then go to the tree from where you took the leaf and bury the parcel of hair beneath it.

To Calm a Fearful Pet

As you probably well know, many of our pets don't like things like lightning, thunder, or 4th of July fireworks. In my house, those things don't bother my dog, Kalli, but the garbage truck petrifies her. She is so afraid of the noise that she whimpers and starts shaking, so I created this spell for trash collection day to ease that fear.

As soon as Kalli hears the truck, she usually comes running to wherever I am. I get down on the floor with her, hold her in my arms, visualize the bright light of protection surrounding us and say the following incantation:

White light, bright light, envelop us in your glow
Take away the fearfulness that makes her feel so low
Surround us with a fluffy cloud of comfort and of ease
Calm her down, remove the fear, of this I ask you please.

So Mote It Be

About halfway though the incantation, I can feel her body begin to relax and the shaking noticeably slows down. By the time the truck is at the end of the block, she's back to her old self again.

Hematite Healing

Hematite is considered to be a good healing and grounding stone. It strengthens the body and improves resistance to life's stresses. It is also considered to be a self-healing stone. If you scratch it then rub the scratch with your fingers, the scratch goes away, so it's a terrific stone to use to aid healing.

You will need:

1 small hematite stone

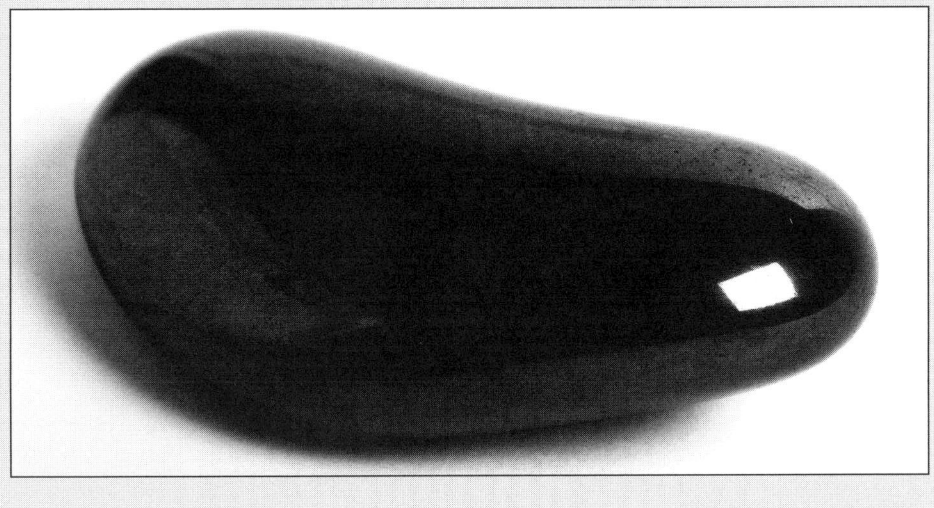

Hold the stone in the palm of your hand and send all of your healing energy into it.

Put the stone down in front of you, then repeat the following incantation:

Precious stone, now go to work
Before this ailment goes berserk
Your healing powers I do ask
To work their magic and complete the task

So Mote It Be

For a dog or cat, sew a small hematite crystal into their collars, making sure there is no way the stone can get dislodged and accidentally swallowed. Tie one onto a bird's cage, place a stone on top of an aquarium, in a horse's saddlebag or anywhere else where it will not be of danger to the animal.

Celebrate New Arrivals

Whether you live on a farm or in the city, our animal friends oftentimes share the joy and miracle of birth with us. The next time you have a newborn in your midst, perform this simple candle spell to welcome them.

You will need:

A pink candle, a green candle, and a gold candle
Rose oil
Myrrh or rose incense
A photo of the newborn
1 rose quartz or lapis lazuli crystal

Anoint the candle with rose oil and then light the incense and the candle.

Place the stone on top of the picture and repeat the following incantation:

I welcome you with all my heart
And bright blessings to you I do impart
From this moment I do pray
That you grow healthy and stronger day by day
And live your life content and free
Of strife and hardship

So Mote It Be

Let the candles burn out completely…unless you must leave the house, in which case, blow out the candles and relight them when you return.

To Protect Animals From Abuse

If there is one thing I despise more than anything else is the abuse of innocent animals. All of God's creatures need to be treated with love and respect, and that certainly includes those in the animal kingdom.

Unfortunately, we can't be there to protect all of the unfortunate creatures who may suffer at the hands of cruel and heartless humans, but we can take action against animal cruelty, whether it be on a personal or global level, with the following spell.

You will need:

A purple candle
Frankincense Incense
A sprig of lavender
Patchouli oil
A quartz crystal
A sharp pin

With the pin, etch your intentions into the candle. Anoint the candle with the oil, place the lavender next to the candle and repeat the following incantation:

Protect all abused creatures from violence and pain
Protect them from those who are filled with disdain
Protect them from anger and hardship and greed
Protect them from those who lie and mislead
May Karma take over with lightning speed
And stop the insanity
Let these creatures be freed

So Mote It Be

This spell is strongest when done on the New Moon.

Pet Protection Bottle

The power of Witch Bottles is undeniable. They have been used for hundreds of years and are used to protect, defend, banish, enhance, or attract. They can also be used to encourage and inspire harmonious energies and blessings. What you put in your bottle depends on your intention, but in this case, the bottle is for protection.

The theory behind a protection bottle is that it serves as a trap for negative energy so you fill it with sharp items, so that the negativity will get stuck on the sharp items and cannot leave.

If you don't have a proper bottle, you may use a jar with a tight fitting lid.

You may use any assortment of sharp items such as:

Old nails
Needles and Pins
Broken Pottery and Broken Glass

I would also toss in some:

Rose Thorns or Cactus Needles
Bay or Basil Leaves
A Dash or Two of Cayenne Pepper or Red Pepper Flakes
A Clove of Garlic

Seal the jar tightly and then use the following incantation:

The sharps and spikes and heat of spice
Will now make this bottle my device
To keep my pet safe from harm
And it will surely work like a charm

So Mote it Be

Traditionally, Witch Bottles are to be buried either under the hearth or at the farthest corner of your property. If neither of those options is available, just make sure you put it somewhere out of plain view and where it will not be disturbed.

Horse Braid Spell

Braiding a horse's mane and tail serves as a protective device to the horse, and this spell has been around forever.

In a sense, this is a form of knot or cord magick. The Witches Ladder is one of the most common forms of this kind of magick. A witch's ladder is a fetish in folk magic or witchcraft that is made from knotted cord or hair. Charms are knotted or braided with specific magical intention into the cords. The number of knots and nature of charms varies with the intended effect.

Many pagans plait the mane and tail into thirteen braids each. Some add straw to the braids, others entwine red ribbons or small bells and charms.

Repeat this simple incantation as you do the braiding:

Safe and sound, my wishes bound
Prayers displayed by my braid
Blessings come from the source
For the safety and well-being of my horse

So Mote It Be

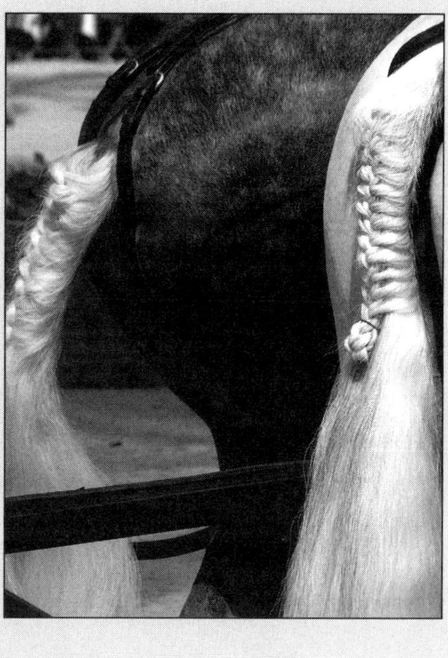

Feather Quill Communication

This spell can be used either for communicating with your pet bird or familiar, or birds in the wild.

You will need:

1 feather that your pet has dropped during molting
(NEVER pluck one out)

Cinnamon incense
A sharp knife
A bottle of violet or purple ink,
(although black ink can be substituted if need be)
A piece of parchment paper
A piece of purple ribbon

Light the incense; then take the feather and sharpen the end of it into a point with the knife.

Dip the newly made quill into the ink and write your message on the parchment.

As the ink is drying, repeat the following incantation:

These words that I do now impart
Are written to you from my heart
A visual image you shall receive
Of what information you are meant to receive
This message is between you and me
As it shall remain

So Mote It Be

When the ink is dried, roll the parchment into a scroll and tie it with the ribbon.

Place the scroll in between the branches and leaves of your favorite tree if the message is for a wild bird. If it is for your pet, place it on your altar.

From the Heart Spell

Whenever my cat Pipsqueak, Bentley the bird, or my dog Kalli don't feel well, or just feel out of sorts, I hold them close to my heart and talk to them quietly. This, of course, was easier with little Bentley or with Pipsqueak than a huge dog, but it seems as though holding a loved one close and letting them feel your heartbeat works wonders.

There is nothing you need as far as tools are concerned. The love in your heart will do the trick. As for the words, those should come from the heart as well. Tell them how much you love them, offer them encouragement, let them know how important they are to you. Say whatever is on your mind in a calm and soothing voice. Bentley liked his neck rubbed when I did this, Pipsqueak loves the cuddles and Kalli likes her chest being rubbed at the same time. You know the things your pets like, so use the physical expressions of love as well as the words.

I usually do this for 5-10 minutes at a time. It's a great way to make both a physical and mental connection for both you and your pet and you will benefit from the experience as well.

To Prevent Nightmares

Just like humans, when pets are stressed, those blissful puppy and kitty dreams sometimes turn to nightmares. Here is a simple spell that will help alleviate their troubled sleep.

> You will need:
>
> 1 obsidian, peridot, or citrine crystal

Hold the crystal in the palm of your hand and transfer your energy to it. Then place you hand, with the stone still inside over your pet's head and repeat the following incantation:

A blissful sleep I wish for you
Happy thoughts will now ensue
Sleep comfortably and trouble free
It shall be done

So Mote It Be

Place the stone on you pet's altar or on your own and use as often as necessary.

HEAVEN

Voyager Prayer

The circle of life cannot be broken. The time between the miracle of birth to the ultimate parting is when we live, love, and learn.

I truly believe that animals sometimes understand the circle better than we do, and while they do not look forward to leaving us, they instinctively know it must be. I think it's important that we let them know that we also understand that they must go, and send them off with a prayer.

Your time has come, my little friend
Your physical life is at its end
Go with the angels and do not fear
Because your spirit will always be near
The bond of love will act as a tether
And keep our hearts always together
With all my love I set you free
May your voyage be blissful

So Mote it Be

Freeze Those Fleas

A freezer binding spell can have many uses. They are normally done on humans, to keep them from bothering others, but as a rule, binding spells should only be used in extreme cases, except when it comes to pests of the insect variety.

> You will need:
>
> A small waterproof container
> A picture or drawing of a flea
> A piece of black thread or string

Hold the picture in both hands and gaze at it while repeating the following incantation:

Pesky flea you're not welcome here
I'm freezing you so you can't come near
Enter this house and you will feel
A bitter cold that will make you reel
If you ride on my pet from outside to in
You'll drop off so quickly it will make your head spin.

So Mote It Be

Fold the paper three times and tie it with black thread or string. Place into the watertight container, fill the container with water, and place in the freezer.

Keep Pets from Wandering Off

Most animals are born with the wanderlust and want to go out and explore, unaware of the dangers that may await them. To keep them from roaming where they shouldn't, try this simple spell.

You will need:

1 brown candle
2 pet treats
A pinch of salt

Light the candle, give your pet a treat and recite the following incantation:

Stay close to home, don't run away
You're safe right here so don't you stray
Your safety is important to me
So here you'll stay

So Mote It Be

Sprinkle your animal's tail with a pinch of salt, and give him/her another treat. Blow out the candle and repeat this spell three nights in a row.

Happy Aquarium Spell

If you dedicate your aquarium (or even a goldfish bowl) to the water gods or goddesses, they will help keep it safe and its inhabitants happy.

If you have a salt water aquarium, you might want to call upon Poseidon or Neptune. For freshwater, try Tethys, Egeria, or Manawydan.

This spell can be cast as you set up a new aquarium or with an existing one.

You will need:

An aquarium or fish bowl with at least one fish
A Pisces or Aquarius amulet

Place the amulet next to the tank and call upon the deity you have chosen to watch over your tank and dedicate it to them by saying:

(Name of deity)
I dedicate this tank in your honor
Please make it a healthy environment for all the lovely creatures living within
Watch over them and keep them safe from harm

So Mote It Be

Vet Guide Invocation

Sometimes when my pets are under the weather, in addition to taking them to their veterinarian, or casting a spell on my own, I call upon a veterinarian spirit guide to assist in their healing. A little divine intervention never hurts!

You will need:

Spirit incense
A white candle
A quartz crystal (to assist in bringing the guide in)
A Chinese Dragon amulet (To offer strength for your pet)

Light the incense and the candle and place the quartz and the dragon between them. Then recite the following invocation:

With love in my heart and the best of intentions, I call upon (pet's name) vet guide to come through and assist him/her in curing this malady. I also invoke other healing beings to come and assist you, be they healing spirits of nature, animal totems, or benevolent elementals. Please join together and offer the divine healing that he/she needs in order to recover quickly and fully.

So Mote It Be

Let the incense and candle burn out on their own. Repeat this invocation as often as you feel necessary.

Note: The dragon amulet must be a Chinese and not European dragon. The Chinese dragon is a symbol of power, strength, and good luck.

Sleep Through The Night Lullaby

Any new pet owner knows that the first few nights of having a new addition in your house, especially a youngster or newborn can be sleepless ones for both you and your new little loved one.

Some people suggest placing a ticking clock in the pet bed to emulate a mother's heart sounds. While you might add one to the spell, I've always found that a lullaby works wonders.

You will need:

A stick of clary sage incense
Soothing music in the background

Light the incense and lie down next to your pet's bed. He/she will pick up on your relaxed mood. Lie quietly next to him/her for a few moments and gently pet him/her and in a calm, quiet voice, recite this lullaby:

The sun has set, the moon is high
It's now time for your lullaby
Your eyes are closing, the Sandman is near
Let your mind be free and clear
Sleep peacefully and trouble free through the night
And wake up when the sun is bright

So Mote It Be

Stay with your pet until he/she dozes off, if possible.

How To Create and Cast Your Own Spell

By using the various appendixes in this book, it's a simple matter to make up your own spells as you see fit. In fact, the best type of spell is one you have created yourself. Just remember that as much energy as you put into your magick, that's as much as you'll get out.

1. First, and most important, is your intention. You must KNOW that you have the power within you.

2. Use meditation to clear you mind of all outside influences before you cast the spell. Remember that negativity within you can change magickal output in unexpected and unpleasant ways.

3. The next step is to focus on your goal. Then look around you and collect items that immediately remind you of your goal. You'll want to enhance the spell's effect with an appropriate scent and/or an appropriate gemstone, amulet, herb, or corresponding candle color. For example, a candle spell for money would require a green candle, a copper coin, a green adventurine or tourmaline gemstone, allspice or cinnamon incense, and perhaps a sun amulet. The amount of accessories you use is up to you.

4. After you've gathered your accessories, prepare a sacred space. Envision yourself surrounded by a sphere of white light.

5. You may also call on a deity or specific element to aid a spell. The four elements are Air (East), Fire (South), Water (West), and Earth (North). Simply stand in the direction associated with the element and politely ask for each Guardian to join you and watch over you during your spell. Then you may invite any other spirits and deities that you wish.

6. If you have a particular deity you want help from, invoke him/her at this time. Otherwise, call upon the God and Goddess and use the phrase, "By your power, through my will." (Some people simply choose to use the Lesser Banishing Ritual before spell casting instead of calling upon the elements or a specific deity. See the Lesser Banishing Ritual at the end of this section.)

7. Then go ahead and cast the spell incorporating all your senses into it and when you're finished, bind the spell. This is a realization that you take full responsibility for the spell and its intent, because when you perform a spell, the energy you have put into it is bound to you. By making the Binding Statement, "So Mote It Be," you are acknowledging the power the spell has and you are redefining your intention.

8. Thank the elemental powers that be; then ground yourself. Sit on the floor and take a few cleansing breaths. Eat a piece of hard candy or chocolate. Visualize small roots growing out of your feet and legs to anchor you to the earth. Stay put until you feel back to normal.

The Lesser Banishing Ritual

The Lesser Banishing can be done at the beginning of the spell casting ritual to clear the area for magickal workings and then again after to discharge the magickal force raised during a ritual. This ritual can be done anywhere, and is useful on the astral to "get rid of" unwanted visitors (i.e. elementals or other etheric beings you run into on the astral).

To perform the ritual, walk around the space that you intend to be encompassed by the ritual, with your wand, athame, or finger "drawing" a circle as you go, starting at the East and going clockwise until you return to the East. There is no set circumference, but all participants and ritual items that you intend to use should be within this circle.

In each of the four quarters, starting with the East, you should now inscribe the banishing pentagram. As each pentagram is completed, you should pause and charge the pentagram by repeating the name of the Goddess. Repeat the name for each direction and each pentagram that you inscribe. East—YHWH (pronounced Ya ho Wah). South—Adonai. West—EHIHE (pronounced ee hee ay). North—AGLA (pronounced ah glah). Return to the East.

Now Invoke the Archangels of the Four Quarters by facing East as you say,

Before me stands Raphael
Behind me stands Gabriel
On my right hand Michael
On my left hand Auriel
For about me shines the pentagram
And above me shines the six-rayed star.

Raising Energy

Raising Energy is the process of gathering energy into yourself and containing it so you may use it in spells, charms, etc. This is one of the most important elements of casting and can be done in a variety of ways. Singing, chanting, dancing, drumming, and visualization are several methods commonly used. Here are some suggestions for raising energy in preparation for your spell work.

White Light

Stand at the altar and imagine a white light flowing into your body through the top of your head. Also feel it coming up through your feet and then feel the energy coming together and forming a ball of light in your chest. Focus completely on building up every bit of energy you have. When you feel as though you have raised all of your energy, relax and proceed with the spell.

After the spell is complete, it is necessary to send out the energy that was raised. This energy is released into the world to create the change you desire. To do this, stand at the altar and imagine the ball of light in your chest once more. Tense your muscles and begin to "push" the energy upward. Then, thrust your arms into the air and exhale, imagining sending this energy out into the air.

Chants and Mantras

Some people prefer to chant or use mantras to raise energy. The chant is usually repeated over and over again, quietly at first, then louder and faster as you go, until the energy reaches the appropriate level to "empower" the workings.

Drumming

Some people like to rhythmically beat a drum for a few minutes. As with chanting, the drum starts slowly and then gets louder and faster.

Energy Ball

Sit in a quiet room and remove all jewelry, and eyeglasses; then hold your hands out in front of you with the palms facing each other. Bring your hands together and rub them vigorously for a few seconds; then slowly begin to separate your hands to about 3 inches apart, keeping them level with each other. At this point you should feel a tingling sensation.

Now slowly bring them back together but don't let them touch. Then once again, slowly pull them apart and then back towards each other. Do this several times.

As your hands go towards and away from each other, you should feel a ball of energy between them. If you don't feel it at first, keep trying.

Once you are able to successfully raise energy between your hands and are comfortable with it, you then can learn to focus your energy by turning your hands towards an object and fill that object with your energy before casting a spell.

Candle Magick

Candle Magick is a very powerful form of magic, yet quite easy to apply. Candle color is very important when performing magick, for each color emits a particular vibration and attracts certain influences.

Any type of candle can be used for spells as long as it has been cleansed and consecrated prior to use. This step removes all the negative energies that the candle has picked up along the way.

To Cleanse and Consecrate the Candle:

Submerge it in sea salt and the ask The Lord and Lady to bless it in your own words.

Dressing the Candle

Before beginning your spell with the consecrated candle, it must be properly dressed. Dressing the candle with oil is as important as any other step.

Use whatever oil you prefer or what a specific spell asks you to use. I use Myrrh oil unless otherwise specified.

The direction you dress the candle is important. To bring something **to you**, rub oil on the candle in a downward motion from top to bottom and to send something **away from** you, rub the oil up from the bottom to the top. Never make a back and forth motion as this defeats the purpose.

You can then dab the remaining oil on your fingers onto your third eye. Then say:

This candle has been consecrated in the name of the Lord and the Lady.
May it burn bright and do my bidding.

Then state your intent or the purpose of the candle and begin your spell.

Candle Colors and Properties

Here are the various candle colors and their magickal properties:

RED

Strength, power, energy, health, vigor, enthusiasm, courage, passion, fertility, protection.

PURPLE/VIOLET

Highly spiritual and traditionally connected to mysticism, inspiration, wisdom, idealism, purification; success, peace; and power. A powerful color to use when working with your familiars.

MAGENTA

A very high vibrational frequency that tends to speed up the outcome of spellwork. This color energizes rituals where immediate action and high levels of power or spiritual healing are required, such as quick changes, or spiritual healing.

BROWN

Aids in emotional stability and balance, eliminates indecisiveness, improves powers of concentration, intuition, and telepathy. Also connects to finding lost objects and pets. Aids in the protection of familiars and household pets as well as animal healing.

INDIGO

Is used to cleanse the spirit and remove fear. Used in rituals that require a deep meditative state, to neutralize another's magick, or to counteract negative energy being sent to you or your pets.

BLUE

Soothing and relaxing in nature, blue is a primary spiritual color, used in rituals to obtain wisdom, tranquility, harmony, peace, inner light, and truth. Connects to inspiration, occult power, protection, understanding, good health, patience, and loyalty. It promotes happiness, laughter, and joviality.

GREEN

Aids good fortune, prosperity, luck, ambition, and success. It is also an emotional soother and balancer, used to counteract greed and jealousy.

SILVER / GRAY

These neutral colors removes negative energy or influences and encourages stability. Useful when pondering complex issues during meditation and in magic; this color often sparks confusion in others. It also negates or neutralizes when needed.

BLACK

When burned for positive purposes, this color opens up the deeper levels of the unconscious. Black is used in rituals to induce a deep meditational state and is good for banishing evil or negativity. Connects to self control, quiet power, and resilience, as it absorbs negativity and destroys it; offers strength and support in spells; protects from retribution and is also an aid during loss.

WHITE

A balance of all the colors, white is great for meditation, healing, spiritual enlightenment, cleansing, clairvoyance, and truth seeking. It also assists with spirit communication, brings peace, and releases positive energy. A white candle may be substituted for any color candle.

GOLD

Allows understanding, brings about fast luck, solar energy, to heal all inner wounds.

Magickal Herbs

Herbs were used for healing and Magick long before they were used as seasonings for food. They were used in potions, incenses, and amulets to ward off evil, attract prosperity, protect children, and women in labor, and to heal illnesses. The following herbs and plants are used by us in casting spells for and about our pets, but some of these are toxic to pets, so please research any that you intend to use fully prior to working with your animal.

ALOE

From the plant or in gel form, aloe is often used on burns and can relieve poison ivy rash. Many dog shampoos use the foaming quality of aloe to help keep a dog's coat clean and shiny. Aloe is also used in a variety of natural flea treatments to help with itching. Ear cleansers are available with aloe vera gel. However, according to the American Society for the Prevention of Cruelty to Animals, the **aloe vera plant is toxic to dogs if ingested**.

AMARANTH (Cockscomb)

Grow angelica in the garden for protection.

ANGELICA ROOT (Archangelica-Angelica)

For protection and also exorcism.

This plant builds female and creative energy, bringing inspiration and helping new ideas to grow and build a foundation. Grow angelica in the garden for protection. Carry the root with you as an amulet. Burn the dried leaves in exorcism rituals. An aromatic herb, it is sometimes used to flavor liquor.

BASIL

For protection, love, healing relationships, courage, fertility, and exorcism.

BAY

For wisdom, protection, and psychic powers.

A wonderful all-purpose herb but **DO NOT TAKE BAY LEAVES INTERNALLY**. This herb is sacred to Apollo, god of healing, poetry, music, light, prophecy, and, surprisingly, plague.

CATNIP

Good for cat magick, familiars, joy, friendship, and love. As incense it may be used to consecrate Magickal tools.

CHAMOMILE

Good in meditation incense, also used for centering, and peace, but if you are growing chamomile in your garden, as many do because it is planted for success, and is sprinkled around the house to dispel negative magick, PLEASE remember that **this plant is toxic to cats, dogs, and horses.**

CINNAMON

For inviting spiritual quests, augmenting power, love, success, psychic work, healing, cleansing, protection, and prosperity.

CLOVE

Used in incense to dispel negativity, psychic vision, and cleansing.

COMFREY

Used for safe travel spells, money drawing, and healing. Comfrey is beneficial for humans to boost the immune system and speed healing, but **it isn't a good herb for dogs**. The alkaloids in comfrey can cause permanent liver damage.

CORIANDER

For the protection of home, peace, incenses for security, longevity and love. While coriander is not considered toxic to pets, the plants do contain a variety of compounds that **can potentially cause some gastrointestinal irritation,** depending on the level of exposure.

DANDELION

For divination, welcoming, and messages.

While dandelions are not considered toxic to pets, I kind of go by the rule that any plant with a milky stem is toxic. Better to be safe than sorry.

FENNEL

For spells relating to purification, protection, and healing. For protection, fennel was hung over the doorway on Midsummer Eve to keep away evil and the seeds put into keyholes to keep out ghosts. An infusion of fennel also makes a good door wash to keep away intruders.

GINGER

Used for power, success, love, and money.

GINSENG

Love, wishes, beauty, and desire.

A stimulant, tonic, and agent for prolonged life. Ginseng is also a mild pain killer, and improves blood circulation. Reported to successfully treat asthma, bronchitis, cancer, flatulence, diabetes, weakness, fever, coughs, and heartburn, and a mild stimulant. In tea form, it helps to relieve stress and moderate heart disease.

GARLIC

Used in spells for protection, healing, courage, and exorcism. Dogs, and especially cats, are sensitive to garlic. We do not know specifically what dosage causes problems, and it is not yet completely known what breeds and age groups are most sensitive to this toxicity, but **gastrointestinal problems and red blood cell damage can occur as a result of feeding garlic to pets.**

JUNIPER BERRIES

Juniper berries purify the aura, clarifies thought, and protects from negativity. The berry is used against anxiety, to improve memory and mental clarity, and for sedation. **But are toxic to both dogs and cats.**

LAVENDER

Aids in spells for sleep, long life, peace, wishes, protection, and purification. Lavender also has strong antiseptic qualities. Witches throw it onto the Midsummer fires as a sacrifice to the ancient Gods. Lavender is a frequent addition to healing sachets, especially bath mixtures, and is added to incense to cause sleep. It is also said to stimulate the immune system and is not harmful to pets.

LEMON

Use for purification and blessings.

MALLOW FLOWERS (Blue)

Useful in Water magick. Blue mallow promotes spiritual healing and peace.It can be incorporated into a dream pillow for soothing nightmares.

MARIGOLD

Aids in prophesy, the psychic, seeing magickal creatures, love, clairvoyance, and dreams. These dried petals are a good incense for consecrating objects used for divination. Petals can also be strewn to consecrate a particular area but be careful to keep the pets away. If your cat eats marigold leaves or stems, she will suffer **mild mouth irritation, possible drooling, tummy pain and diarrhea. The new leaves and stems are toxic to dogs as well.**

MARJORAM

For protection, love, healing.

Give marjoram to a grieving person who has lost a pet to help alleviate sorrow.

MINT (SPEARMINT and PEPPERMINT)

Mint is used in spells for healing, strength, augment power and luck.

MYRRH

Excellent for blessing objects, lifting energy, spiritual growth and focus, but it can be toxic in large doses so keep this and all other essential oils away from your pets.

MYRTLE

Used for protection. Throwing this magick herb into a fire was believed to make the face of one's future mate appear in the smoke. This could also be potentially true when looking to mate your pet.

NETTLE

Used to avert danger, for protection, and for healing. It is great for some spellwork, but **stinging nettles can injure your pets** so it is advisable to keep them out of your garden and watch for them while walking your pets.

ORANGE PEEL

It is said to communicate the joy of angels to human beings. It lifts the spirits, helps the confused find direction and gives new life to spiritual yearnings. Because of its color, orange peel also makes a handy symbol for gold in spell work.

PEPPERCORNS (White)

For granting wishes, building protection, strength, confidence, and inventiveness. Pepper helps with focus and with clarifying thoughts, lessens anxiety, lifts mild depression, levels hormone-induced mood swings, and calms anxiety.

PINE

Attunement to nature, centering, cleansing, healing, productivity, and purification against illness. For magic, pine is best suited for its aromatic qualities of bringing one back into balance, and enhancing connection with the natural world. Pine cones are not poisonous to your pets per se, but **if swallowed they can definitely cause problems.** If parts of the pine cone is swallowed and not passed in the stool, surgery may be needed to be cut open to get them out.

ROSE

Used in spells for friendship, harmony luck, protection, psychic power, and divination. Roses are high in vitamin C and are safe if ingested by pets, but **thorns either swallowed or poked into the skin can cause infection** if left untreated, as well as painful.

ROSEMARY

Improves the memory and also used for power, healing, and protection, and enhances intellectual activities. Burn rosemary and juniper as a healing and recuperation incense.

STAR ANISE

Burned for clairvoyance and to increase psychic awareness. This herb is great for New Moon work, since it is dark. Can be put under the pillow in order to dream of someone far away, and can also be added to mojo bags that you make up for yourself and your pets.

TONKA BEANS

Used in spells for courage. Tonka beans are sometimes thrown into a river to make dreams come true. These should never be ingested because they are toxic to both man and beast.

WORMWOOD

For protection, vengeance through sorcery.

It is considered to be a good treatment for injuries done by "martial creatures" such as wasps, hornets, or scorpions, repels bugs from stored clothing. The seeds were once taken internally to get rid of worms, hence the name. Wormwood is a traditional de-worming herb. It is however too strong on pets and wormwood **should only be used with extreme caution under strict holistic veterinarian advice**.

YARROW

For courage, love, psychic abilities, divination. A powerful incense additive for divination. **It is toxic to cats, dogs, and horses.**

YEW

Associated with death, burning yew as an incense is still a traditional means for raising the dead and thus in a sense, entrapping them.

Yew is commonly recommended for making runes, wands, and bows. **Yew is exceedingly poisonous. Ingesting it in any form can easily be fatal.**

Magickal Gemstones

Gemstones are nice to wear, but they also have uses that aren't just decorative. They are used in spells, carried in pockets and I have a bowl of select gemstones on my desk. Here is a list of the most common gemstones and their magickal properties which can be applied to our pets and their magickal needs as well:

AGATE
Good for transmutation, helps with the emotion of acceptance, gives a mellow, blended aspect, simplistic, has stabilizing effect, helps physical endurance.

AGATE/BLUE LACE
Brings higher states of consciousness, balances psychic centers, aids depression, despair and stubbornness, balances emotions, calms the mind.

AGATE/BOTSWANA
Increases physical strength, enhances stamina, and endurance, protects sensitivity when weak.

AGATE/CARNELIAN
Stimulates energy, physical power, and courage.

AGATE/FIRE
Enhances all essences, grounds and balances, sexual & heart chakra binder, burns energy.

AGATE/LACE
Helps alleviate depression, despair and stubbornness, helps stabilize emotions, calms the mind while energizing the body.

AGATE/MOSS
Emotional priorities, mental priorities, binds the energies of nature to bring you in tune with the flora and fauna, helps increase healing, long life, fertility.

AGATE/PICTURE:

Left and right brain imbalances. Apathy is eased.

ALABASTER

Enhances the skills employed for providing service to man, provides maturity and bestows composure during times of stress.

AMAZONITE

Strengthens physical stamina.

AMBER

Eccentric behavior, anxiety, general healing, and happiness, absorbs negative energy, very grounding and protective.

AMETHYST

Good for left brain imbalances, edginess, facilitates healing, psychic insight, stimulates third eye, enhances dream state, spiritual guidance, calming the mind.

AQUAMARINE

Alleviates fear, calms nerves, offers mental clarity.

ARROWHEAD/FLINT

Warrior energy, connecting with Native American traditions, sharpness, truth, protection, tool.

ARROWHEAD/BROWN

Grounding, anchoring to earth.

AVENTURINE

Eliminates fear, positive attitude, motivation perception and foresight heals and stabilizes.

AZURITE

Dissolves fear and transforms it into understanding, calming, aids detoxification.

BERYL

A good cure for both laziness and hiccups.

BERYL/GOLDEN

Wisdom. Intellectual stimulation, joy.

BERYL/GREEN (Aquamarine)

Purification, healing prosperity.

BLOODSTONE/HELIOTROPE

All-purpose healer and cleanser.

BOJI STONE

Aligns all of the subtle bodies and both balances and aligns the chakras, removes energy blockages.

CALCITE/GOLDEN

Mental stimulation, concentration, joy, lightness.

CARNELIAN

Grounding, stimulates curiosity and initiative, provides sense of stability, energy, emotional balance.

CELESTITE

Crystal of the heavens, offers ethereal energy.

CHALCEDONY

Works against melancholy, stimulates maternal feelings in new mothers.

CHALCENDONY ROSE

The Goddess Stone, the Divine Mother, female power, womb energy, opening the heart, and compassion.

CHRYSOBERYL

Opens and activates the crown chakra, stone of immortality, assisting one to overcome and to progress toward excellence.

CHRYSOCOLLA

Used for emotional balance and comfort, alleviates fear and nervous tension, facilitates clairvoyance, amplifies thought, strength, healing, opens the heart and throat chakra.

CHRYSOLITE

Inspiration, prophecy.

CHRYSOPGRASE

Promotes sexual organ strength.

CITRINE QUARTZ

Cleanses vibrations in the atmosphere, eliminates self-destructive tendencies.

CLEAR QUARTZ

Transmitter and amplifier of healing energy and clarity, balance, channeler of universal energy and unconditional love, all purpose healer, programmable, brings good health and balance, use for healing, meditation, knowledge, clear thinking and protection, strengthens all other stones when in tandem with them.

CORAL

Protection on or near water, protection against nightmares and evil eye, dispels fear and depression.

DIAMOND

Symbolizes the central sun of the solar system, insures love and harmony and dispels anger.

DOLOMITE

Relieves sorrow.

ELIAT STONE

Antidepressant.

EMERALD

Transmits balance, healing and patience, increases psychic and clairvoyant abilities, meditation, keener insight into dreams.

EPIDOTE

Enhances keen perception, stimulates participation and interaction, and supplements personal power.

FLUORITE

Improves concentration, balances polarities, third eye center, improves memory and concentration, eases anger and desperation, "the student stone" helps assimilate information, mental capacity and intellect.

FELDSPAR

Assists one in locating that which has been misplaced and in discovering and understanding messages from within and without of the self.

FRESH WATER PEARLS

The Divine Mother, feminine, compassion, purity, beauty.

GARNET/RHODOLITE

Body strength, energy, endurance, increases positive vibrations and dispels all negativity, increases sex drive, increases well being.

GARNET/SPESSARTINE

Works against bad dreams, depression and anger, increases self esteem.

GRAPHITE

Used during healing to enhance the energy transfer from a healer to the subject of the healing (as in Reiki), excellent in wands, also the stone of personal freedom, providing impetus for one to take charge of ones life.

GOLDEN TIGER EYE

A great confidence builder.

GOLDSTONE (glass with flecks of copper)

Honesty, relaxation, and sharing, transmitter stone, calming and refreshing.

HEMATITE

Self esteem, augments meridian flows, dissolves negative energy, works as a shield of amore to ward off accidents, illness, and evil eye.

HOWLITE

Good luck if worn or carried, protection at night.

JADE

Strengthens the body, aids in longevity, ancient love attracting stone, wisdom.

JASPER/GREEN

General healer, helps with clairvoyance, balances healers' aural fields.

JASPER/PICTURE/LEOPARD

Great for the immune system, over-activity in dream state and hallucinations. Enables you to work with heavy negativity, stabilizes mood swings, reduces fears and insecurities, protection, grounding.

JASPER/RED

Enhances love and passion, helps you work with heavy negativity, reduces fears and insecurities, beneficial for blood circulation.

JASPER/YELLOW

Enhances love and passion, helps you work with heavy negativity, reduces fears and insecurities, beneficial for blood circulation.

JET

Alignment of lower spine.

KUNZITE

Good for emotional equilibrium and self esteem.

LABRADORITE

Opening third eye, psychic vision, sealing holes in aura.

LAPIS LAZULITE

Insight, strengthens psychic awareness, induces courage, protects, aids healing, purifies, calms and de-stresses, improves emotional clarity and wisdom, attracts spiritual love, frontal lobe stimulation, melancholy, penetrates subconscious blockages, mental and spiritual cleanser, eliminates old and negative emotions, used with other healing stones, thought form amplification.

MALACHITE

Draws out impurities on all levels, balances left and right brain functions, evil eye protector, all-purpose healer.

MOONSTONE

Soothes and balances the emotions, helps eliminate fear of "feeling," encourages inner growth and strength, aids peace, harmony, and psychic abilities, aligns the vertebrae. Opens psychic centers, aids in hormone balancing, aids will power. Sacred to the Goddess.

MOTHER OF PEARL

Clarifies feelings, stabilizing.

OBSIDIAN

Protects the gentle from being abused.

OBSIDIAN/SNOWFLAKE

Unhexing stone, wear or carry to remove curse spells, protects from negativity.

OBSIDIAN/APACHE TEAR

Used to comfort in times of grief.

ONYX

Objective thinking, spiritual inspiration, control of emotions and passions, helps eliminate negative thinking, apathy, stress, protects against draining by others, guards against evil eye, negativity and danger at night.

OPAL

One of the most powerful and magical of all stones, contains the powers of all colors, very good luck, psychic awareness, astral projection, money and power.

OPAL/CHERRY

Wards off depression, apathy, lethargy. Enhances intuition and joy.

OPAL/DARK

Aids in depression.

PEARL

Eliminates emotional imbalances, most powerful when worn at night, speeds love vibrations and attracts love and good fortune, attracts health, courage and physical strength.

PEARL/SEA

Feminine energy, Divine Mother, purity, compassion, truth, protection, beauty.

PERIDOT

Protects against nervousness, helps alleviate spiritual fear, aids in healing hurt feelings and bruised egos, incurs strength and physical vitality, aligns subtle bodies, amplifies other vibrational energies and positive emotional outlook. Clear seeing, problem solving, healer of spirit and physical body, attracts money and luck, protects from stage fright, increases fearlessness and strong will, aids liver functions.

PYRITE

Helps with nervous exhaustion, grounding.

PUMICE

Reminder for one not to "sink" into despair when faced with "heavy" problems. Combats abrasive character traits and alleviates negative attitudes.

RHODOCHROSITE

Works against nightmares and hallucinations, clears the solar plexus of blocked energy, great for unconditional love and forgiveness, evil eye protection.

RHODONITE

Alleviates anxiety, confusion, and mental unrest, promotes calm, self worth, confidence, and enhanced sensitivity, restores physical energy, enhances love and passion.

RHYOLITE

Balances emotions, self worth, enhances capacity to love, aligns emotional and spiritual bodies, stimulates clarity of self expression.

ROSE QUARTZ

Opens the heart chakra, love and self-acceptance. Healer of emotional wounds, dissipates anger and tension, a stone of unconditional love, healing, and opening the heart, maturing, and inner peace.

ROYAL AZEL (SUGALITE OR LUVALITE)

Increases general understanding, protects against negative vibrations, helps one gain power to balance the physical body.

RUBY

Heart chakra, balances love and all spiritual endeavors, self esteem.

RUTILATED QUARTZ (clear crystal w/gold colored threads)

Among the strongest healing stones, strength, balance. Leads you in a positive direction.

SAPPHIRE

Spiritual enlightenment, inner peace, mental illness, antidepressant, aids personal expression.

SCARAB

Various stones, Ancient Egyptian symbol of Sacredness, good luck, protection, but mostly eternal life.

SARDONYX

Mental self control, depression, anxiety and especially for grief.

SMITHSONITE

Eases fear of interpersonal relationships, merges astral and emotional bodies, balances perspective.

SMOKY QUARTZ

Cleanses and protects the astral field, draws out distortion on all levels, good for handling hyperactivity and excess energy, grounding.

SODALITE

Works against oversensitivity, helps intellectual understanding of a situation, awakens third eye, cleanses the mind, heals stress, anxiety, nervousness, anger and fear, helps mind to release guilt, brings peaceful sleep.

SPINEL

A powerful general healerd.

SANDSTONE

Assists one to maintain strength against the distractions of the mind, providing for balancing of one's reality, promotes clarity in thought and sight.

TIGERS EYE

Works at grounding, combines with the earth and sun for practical decision making and creativity, inner strength, self confidence, courage, worn for protection from danger.

TOPAZ

Balances emotions, calms passions, spiritual rejuvenation, releases tension, feelings of joy.

TOPAZ/BLUE

Calming, peaceful, protection when on or near the water, protects against envy, disease, and injury.

TOPAZ/IMPERIAL

Golden light, warmth, manifestation, abundance.

TOURMELINE

Dispels fear, negativity, and grief, calms nerves, concentration, and eloquence improved, raises vibrations, charisma, universal law, tranquil sleep and attracts money.

TOURMELINE/BLACK

Works against anxiety and disorientation, raises altruism, deflects negativity, neutralizes distorted energies, protection, weaving light into aura.

TOURMALINE/RUBELLITE

Creativity, fertility, balances passive or aggressive nature.

TURQUOISE

Master healer, protects against environmental pollutants, subtle body alignment and strengthening, creative expression, communication with spirit. Used by Native Americans for protection against danger, accidents and evil. Promotes harmony.

TRILOBITE

Wisdom.

ZEBRA MARBLE

Kept in the home to protect the household, wear for personal protection.

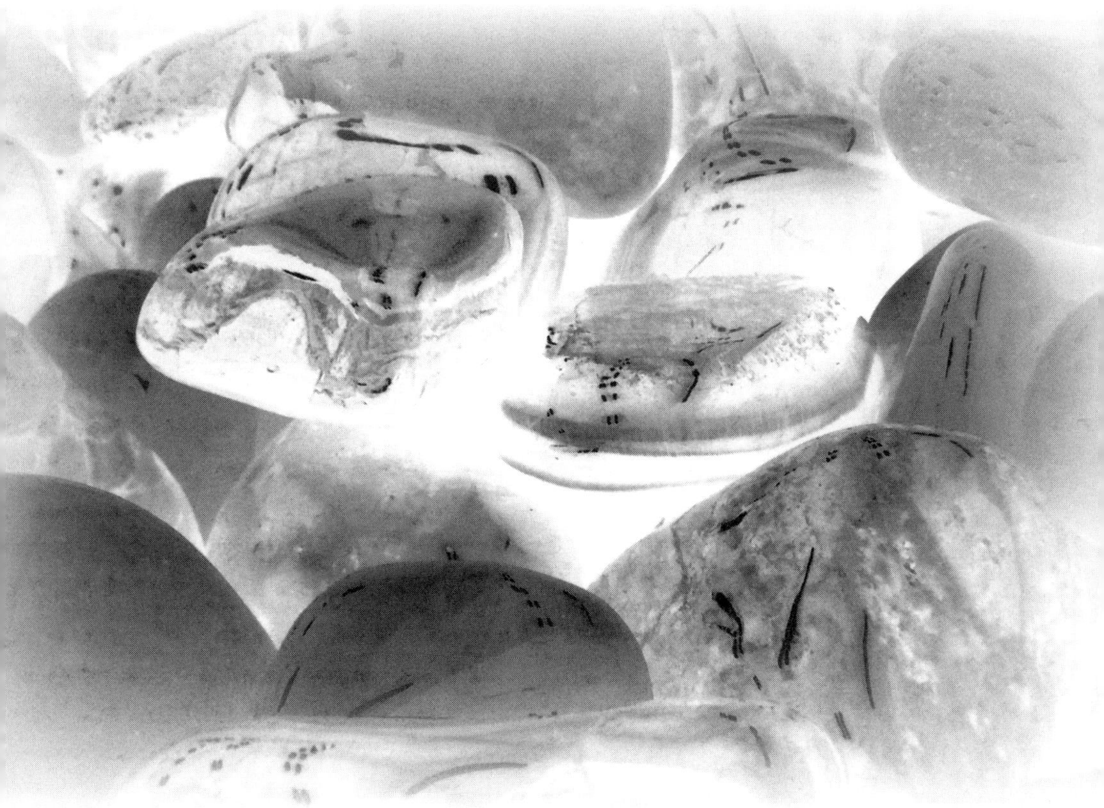

Magickal Properties of Incense

It was an ancient belief that the smoke of incense carried one's prayers up to the Gods. Incense-burning creates a certain atmosphere or vibes which add immeasurably to a Magickal ritual. It is another important ingredient to help achieve the ultimate Magickal power.

Incense is often burned prior to magical workings. The fragrant smoke purifies the area of negative, disturbing vibrations and helps create the appropriate mental state necessary for the successful practice of Magick.

The properties of the particular fragrances listed below are the same for both incense and their corresponding essential oils if you are using the oils for candle magick or to anoint various magickal tools.

ACACIA
Burned with Sandalwood to stimulate the psychic powers.

AFRICAN VIOLET
Burned for protection and to promote spirituality within the home.

ALLSPICE
Burned to attract both good luck and money.

ALTHEA
Burned for protection and to stimulate the psychic powers.

AMBER
Healing and balancing. Strengthens the aura.

BAYBERRY
Protection and control.

CARNATION
Protection, strength and healing.

CEDARWOOD

Purification, healing and to unhex.

CHERRY

Sacred to Venus, this will attract and stimulate love.

CINNAMON

Purify, stimulate, and draw money.

CLARY SAGE

Mental and emotional stress. Encourage sleep, uplift spirits.

CLOVE

Stimulates, reduces stress, and enhances memory.

COCONUT

Burned for protection.

DRAGON'S BLOOD

To dispel negativity, exorcise evil supernatural entities, attract love, and restore male potency.

FRANKINCENSE

Calming. Used for blessings and purifications, to dispel negativity, purify magickal spaces, protect against evil, aid meditation, induce psychic visions, attract good luck, and honor, Pagan deities, meditation, consecration, to attract success and astral strength.

GARDENIA

Attracts love. Restores peace and protection. Calming, soothing and healing.

GINGER

Success and empowerment.

GINSENG ROOT

Burned to keep wicked spirits at bay, and for protection against all forms of evil.

HIGH JOHN

Strength, confidence, and prosperity.

HONEYSUCKLE

For prosperity, assist in weight loss and heighten psychic ability.

JASMINE

For luck in general, especially in matters related to love or money. Relaxing, peaceful, spiritual.

LAVENDER

Antidepressant. Calming and healing, physically and mentally, balancing, helps insure restful sleep, immune builder and for love.

LEMON

Psychic and mental clarity.

LILAC

Warding off and to soothe, increase the psychic powers and to attract harmony into one's life.

LOTUS

High spiritual vibration, healing. Opening, elevating, and protection.

MINT

Increase sexual desire, exorcise evil supernatural entities, conjure beneficial spirits. Also possesses strong healing vibrations and protective powers.

MOONFIRE

Grounding, self love, growth, and inspiration.

MUSK

Courage and vitality. Excites passionate love, promotes sexual attraction, and intense desire.

MYRRH

Protection, healing, spirituality and purification, meditation, healing and unhexing, aids in meditation rituals, consecrations.

NAG CHAMPA

Can be used in any ritual; it is very metaphysical in property.

ORANGE BLOSSOM

Increase energy and joy of life, purification, overcomes depression, calming to stomach, good for dry skin and wrinkles.

PASSION FLOWER

Peace of mind and relations, aids sleep, soothes trouble and problems, brings calm to the home.

PATCHOULI

Love, growth, mastery. Also used for attraction and fertility.

PINE

Grounding, strength, and cleansing, purification, to banish negative entities, returns hexes to their senders.

ROSE

Love, peace, harmony, house blessing, strength, increase courage, induce prophetic dreams, and attract love.

ROSEWOOD

Balancing, eases stress and tension, heightens self-confidence.

SACRED SPACE

Used to sanctify your surroundings.

SAGE

Wisdom, purification and clarity, protection against all forms of evil, aids in healing the body.

SANDALWOOD

All-purpose. Purification and healing. Granting of wishes. Spirituality.

SPICEWOOD

Fiery, multipurpose. Catalyzed for success, luck, love, protection, and healing.

SPEARMINT

For healing, love, and to soothe.

SPIRIT

Attracts spirit guides, raises energy level.

STRAWBERRY

Love and luck.

SWEET CLOVER

Love and faithfulness.

SWEET PEA

Attraction and friendship.

THYME

Burned for the purification of magickal spaces prior to rituals, to aid in healing, and to attract good health.

VANILLA

Stimulate amorous appetites, restore lost energy, jogs memory.

VIOLET
Protection, luck, and love.

VIOLET AND ROSE
Love, peace, harmony, lifts the heart, sedating, healing.

WHITE JASMINE
Used for inspiration, purification, confidence, rejuvenation, and liberation.

YLANG-YLANG
Euphoric and harmonizing.

Kenny Kingston on Pet Grief

The most difficult challenge in loving a pet is eventually having to say goodbye. But according to legendary Psychic to the Stars, Kenny Kingston, "The most important thing to remember is that they are not gone forever. We'll definitely see them again. Our pets are our unconditional friends forever, without question, and even when that beloved friend is taken away from your everyday life, you never, ever lose them in spirit.."

"I have an unbelievable amount of clients who come to me when they lose their beloved pets," says Kingston, "and most of them are a little embarrassed at being so emotional when they ring up, but they shouldn't be, because you *should* grieve, by all means, just as you would for a person, and sometimes even more so because unlike some humans, an animal will never, never, betray you. All they ask from us is a little bit of food and a lot of love."

Kenny suggests that the best way to get over the grief is to cry. "Cry, and remember that the mourning process is different from person to person. Nobody can put a time limit on grief. Just don't be selfish. As with human spirits, animals need time to make the transition. The longer you grieve, the longer you will hold them here on the earth plane. At some point, you need to say to your pet, 'Go on now, and enjoy yourself. I won't grieve for you anymore, but I will pray for you that you're safe.'"

Once a pet has passed over and finally adjusts to being on the other side, Kingston says they often come back for a visit. A recent personal appearance more than proves that the loving bond between humans and their pets holds no boundaries.

"Not long ago, I was performing at the Cinegrill at The Hollywood Roosevelt Hotel," Kingston recalls. "It was my closing night and the room was absolutely packed. I took my final bow, and usually never do an encore. But for some reason, I was drawn to this lady who was seated alone at a table way in the back. I walked over to her and said, 'Ouzoo said to say hello, and he is right there at your feet.' The woman burst into such a happy smile flowing with tears and said, 'Oh, Kenny, I've come all the way from Kansas City to see you. I saw in a California newspaper that you were going to be at The Roosevelt and there were no seats available. I called and pleaded with the manager for a table because tonight is Ouzoo's first anniversary of passing away, and nothing could have made me happier than what you just told me.'"

While Kenny was instrumental in reuniting Ouzoo with his owner, he says that people don't always need to go to such great lengths to know that our little loved ones are around. It's as simple as looking for the signs. "A sensitive person might get a sense of their pet being there by seeing a shadow or feeling an invisible nudge. Some animals will be a little bit more overt in getting your attention, but don't worry about not noticing them. They'll make their presence known to you in a variety of ways. For example, if you have other pets and you've just filled their water bowl, you might hear the water being lapped up even if your pets are nowhere near it. Or, you might notice a toy on the floor moving all by itself. Sometimes," he continues, "one of your other pets may seem as though they're playing with an imaginary friend when actually it's playing with a spirit animal.."

Kingston suggests that you can also initiate a visit by simply using your pet's picture, any type of unscented red candle, and their favorite treat. "Burn the candle next to the picture, and put the treat as a sort of offering," says Kingston. "Then simply say, 'Please come through and let me know that you are all right.' I promise you that even though it may not happen right then and there, eventually you'll be greeted with that familiar meow or bark to let you know they're around."

Rainbows Bridge

There is nothing easy about losing a pet. The heartache and grief stays with us forever, but knowing that our little loved ones are never far away is comforting, and one of the best ways to keep them close is *Rainbows Bridge*, a virtual home for your departed baby. Whether furry, feathered or scaled, all are welcome. Create a Rainbow Residency which you care for as the Guardian of your baby's memory.

In addition to your own pet memorial, the website offers a Pet Loss Grief Support Center, a Monday Candle Lighting Ceremony where people who have lost a Furbaby around the world take time to say a prayer for their departed friend, E-sympathy cards, pet poems and stories, New Beginnings, where the focus is on how to provide the best care for those Furry Friends still sharing their days with you, and so much more.

Enter your beloved Fur Baby as a Rainbow Resident... until the day comes when you meet once again and cross over the Rainbows Bridge together.

Just this side of heaven is a place called Rainbows Bridge.

When an animal dies that has been especially close to someone here, that pet goes to Rainbows Bridge. There are meadows and hills for all of our special friends so they can run and play together. There is plenty of food, water and sunshine, and our friends are warm and comfortable.

All the animals who had been ill and old are restored to health and vigor. Those who were hurt or maimed are made whole and strong again, just as we remember them in our dreams of days and times gone by. The animals are happy and content, except for one small thing; they each miss someone very special to them, who had to be left behind.

They all run and play together, but the day comes when one suddenly stops and looks into the distance. His bright eyes are intent. His eager body quivers. Suddenly he begins to run from the group, flying over the green grass, his legs carrying him faster and faster.

You have been spotted, and when you and your special friend finally meet, you cling together in joyous reunion, never to be parted again. The happy kisses rain upon your face; your hands again caress the beloved head, and you look once more into the trusting eyes of your pet, so long gone from your life but never absent from your heart.

Then you cross Rainbows Bridge together....

Author unknown

Bentley 1984-2010

Resources

Marla Brooks
www.marlabrooks.com
www.myspace.com/marlab717

Willie Windwalker Gibson
spiritly.fatcow.com/windwalker/index.html

Victoria Gross
www.tarotla.com

Kenny Kingston
www.kennykingston.org

Rainbow Bridge
www.rainbowsbridge.com

Dinah Roseberry
roseberrybooks.com
www.schifferghosts.com

Reverend Tim Shaw
blackcatlounge@yahoo.com

Bibliography

Andrews, Ted. *Animal Speak.* Llewellyn Publications; 1Woodbury, MN, 1996.

Brooks, Marla. *Workplace Spells.* Schiffer Publishing. Atglen, PA 2009.

Farmer, Steven. *Power Oracle Cards*. Hay House; Carlsbad, CA. 2006.

Heindal, Max. *Rosicrucian Cosmo-Conception.* Publisher Unknown.

Roseberry, Dinah. *Psychic Pets, Solving Paranormal Mysteries*. Schiffer Publishing. Atglen, PA 2009.

Sams, Jamie and David Carson. Medicine Cards. Bear and Company. Rochester, VT. 1988.

Animal Quotes

"The purity of a person's heart can be quickly measured by how they regard animals."

~Anonymous

"A house is not a home without a pet."

~ Anonymous

"The greatness of a nation and its moral progress can be judged by the way its animals are treated."

~Mahatma Gandhi

"Love the animals: God has given them the rudiments of thought and joy untroubled."

~Fyodor Dostoyevsky

"Animals are such agreeable friends – they ask no questions, they pass no criticisms."

~George Elliot

"I care not for a man's religion whose dog and cat are not the better for it."

~Abraham Lincoln

"It is an important and popular fact that things are not always what they seem. For instance, on the planet Earth, man had always assumed that he was more intelligent than dolphins because he had achieved so much – the wheel, New York, wars and so on – whilst all the dolphins had ever done was muck about in the water having a good time. But conversely, the dolphins had always believed that they were far more intelligent than man – for precisely the same reasons."

~Douglas Adams
The Hitch-Hiker's Guide to the Galaxy

"The kind man feeds his beast before sitting down to dinner."

~Hebrew Prover

"I have been studying the traits and dispositions of the 'lower animals' (so called) and contrasting them with the traits and dispositions of man. I find the result humiliating to me."

~Mark Twain
Letters from the Earth, 1907

"To insult someone we call him 'bestial,' for deliberate cruelty and nature, 'human' might be the greater insult."

~Isaac Asimov
Isaac Asimov's Book of Science and Nature Quotations, 1988

"I don't believe in the concept of hell, but if I did, I would think of it as filled with people who were cruel to animals."

~Gary Larson

"I am in favor of animal rights as well as human rights. That is the way of a whole human being."

~Abraham Lincoln

"The worst sin towards our fellow creatures is not to hate them, but to be indifferent to them. That's the essence of inhumanity."

~George Bernard Shaw

"If you have men who will exclude any of God's creatures from the shelter of compassion and pity, you will have men who will deal likewise with their fellow men."

~St. Francis of Assisi

"God made all the creatures and gave them our love and our fear, to give sign, we and they are His children, one family here."

~Robert Browning

"If a dog will not come to you after having looked you in the face, you should go home and examine your conscience."

~Woodrow Wilson

"The love of all living creatures is the most noble attribute of man."

~Charles Darwin

"Until one has loved an animal, a part of one's soul remains unawakened."
~Anatole France~